CHINA
AFTER THE
CULTURAL
REVOLUTION

CHINA AFTER THE CULTURAL REVOLUTION

A SELECTION FROM

*The Bulletin
of the Atomic Scientists*

RANDOM HOUSE

NEW YORK

First Printing

Copyright © 1969 by Educational Foundation for Nuclear Science

9 8 7 6 5 4 3 2

Library of Congress Catalog Card Number: 72-89701

Manufactured in the United States of America
by The Colonial Press Inc., Clinton, Mass.

Designed by Vincent Torre

Contents

Foreign Policy

Science and Technology

CHINA
AFTER THE
CULTURAL
REVOLUTION

Where China Stands Now: An Introduction

Dick Wilson

A Western diplomat who had the unusual experience of being stationed in Peking during both the Communist takeover and early years of the People's Republic of China, and during the Cultural Revolution of the past three years, states firmly that the second revolution was fiercer and more far-reaching in its effects than the first. Since the earlier "liberation" from the Nationalists of Chiang Kai-shek, Mao Tse-tung has carried China through a second "liberation," this time from the Communist Party which he himself helped to found and led to victory in 1949.

Our surprise at this turn of events must stand as an indictment of those analysts and commentators who wanted us to believe, during the heyday of surface harmony in the Peking leadership of the 1950s, that seventeen million members of the Chinese Communist Party were working, thinking, and speaking as one. What we have had to come to terms with since Mao Tse-tung called on Chinese youth to "Bombard the Headquarters" (in his own first big-character poster of August 5, 1966) is that the Chinese Communists are not superhuman, and that the Chinese people are not subhuman: the for-

mer can and do betray their ideals, the latter can and do
disobey.

It is doubtful whether more than a small fraction of the
seventeen million Party members in China have any real
grasp of Marxist-Leninist theory. Most of them are incapable of altering overnight the ways and mores of mil-
lennia. We were told by some commentators a decade ago
that a quarter of mankind had been transformed into a
vast prison camp of Orwellian dimensions, where total
obedience to the *diktat* of a mad emperor was the only
rule of life. The truth is less exciting, less flattering
to those in Peking who wanted change, less damning of
those who have tried to govern China during these past
two decades.

The China that Mao inherited in 1949 was, perhaps,
tired of strife and war, ready to forego debating and submit to the leadership of a group of men who at least knew
their own minds, were not corrupt, and had some constructive ideas about how to rescue peasant life from the
cumulative misery and degradation of centuries of national decline. It was a China ready to be united, ready
perhaps to sacrifice something in the interests of progress.
But it was at bottom, after all, nothing more or less than
five or six hundred million human beings, prisoners of
their education and social tradition, victims of selfishness
and every other human weakness.

It should not have surprised us that in the end the
Communist Party, the iconoclasts and reformers of the
1940s, should have gradually become the privileged
elite—bureaucratic and out of touch with the common
man—of the 1960s. It should not have surprised us that
twenty years of Communist rule should have left so
many large pockets of frustration, envy, and discontent
where a political leader could find effective allies against
the Party machine. It should not have surprised us that

the definite, if modest, measure of improvement in Chinese life since 1949 should have created an appetite for individualism and independence rather than more hunger for self-abasement and sacrifice. It should not have surprised us that the recovery of self-confidence and stability among one in four of the human race should have strengthened the instinct for autonomy at every level— household, family, village, county, province, and region —and rendered China progressively more difficult to rule from one single desk in Peking.

The only thing that should legitimately have surprised us is that the acknowledged architect of the new China, the grand old man who is its conscience, its guide, its embodiment and symbol, should at the age of seventy-two have taken up the cudgels against his colleagues, against a majority in the Party he had nurtured, and organized a crusade across the length and breadth of China for his own policies. Even this might conceivably have been anticipated by those who have studied the lives of great men and noticed their tendency in old age to kick away the scaffolding upon which they have climbed to eminence, as if to see whether they could not keep their place without it.

No Fundamental Change

The first point, therefore, from which to start an appraisal of where China stands today after all this turmoil is a recognition that, contrary to the propaganda of the Communists, ironically parroted by some of their most hostile critics in the West, China has not fundamentally changed over the past twenty years. She has recovered a great deal of poise, self-respect, and adequacy of living standards, but these by themselves would tend merely to reinforce the pre-existing social fabric.

Communism has tried to unravel and reweave that fabric, and it has set in motion reforms that over a fairly long period will indeed change and modernize the Chinese character, the Chinese way of life, and the Chinese outlook on the world. One of the most fascinating areas of scholarly research these days is a preliminary assessment of the ways in which Chinese culture *has* changed under Communism. But the distance covered so far is slight, and it is still easier to detect the similarities with the past than the departures from it.

I myself had the experience of touring Communist China in 1964, after years of digesting both the flamboyant claims of the Peking press and the hostile Western indictments of Mao for destroying the family and pushing the Chinese peasant too roughly, too forcibly, and too fast into a not entirely wanted modernity. To my astonishment, the visit to China was like a journey back into the eighteenth century. Unlike anywhere in the West or in the industrialized Soviet bloc, unlike those Westernized or developed pockets of Africa and Asia which foreign visitors frequent, the mighty expanses of China proved a haven of old-fashioned courtesy and patience. Everyone has time for everyone else, no sense of urgency is apparent, and the principal content of daily life is the proper conduct of encounters with neighbors, friends, visitors, and officials.

There is virtually no traffic on the roads, and the arrival of a traveler from abroad, however unimportant or from whatever country, is the occasion for very real excitement and interest among most of the people he brushes shoulders with. The sole railway station and only airport of the city from which these 700 million people are administered had respectively, in 1964, two trains

and one international flight leaving every day. It was
utterly impossible to remember, from within China, that
this was a country whose name alone was enough to fur-
row brows and catch heartbeats in the Pentagon and
State Department.

Facing the Realities

The fact that on special occasions a show of frenzy can
be put on, a massive display organized to make Hitler's
parades look like a Sunday school outing, does not alter
the general tenor of Chinese life. It is these special, and
specially contrived, events which we in the West see on
our TV screens and which frighten us. But the real China
that still exists beneath these occasional applications of
theatrical make-up is the teen-age Red Guard, fresh from
the provinces. In the bus, after the day-long rally saluted
by Chairman Mao, he relaxes from his moment of history
and inquires about the Western reporter's suiting, his
opinion of China, his monthly wages, and his taste
for Chinese food. The warm smile that accompanies such
exchanges is more natural than the grimace of hatred
which the same boy will produce to order when the evils
of American imperialism are being ceremonially condemned.

I am not trying to argue that China is naive, simple,
unproblematic, and merely misunderstood. China is extremely complex, is becoming more so, and we should be
wary of oversimplified responses whether they are urged
on us by her friends or foes. But we should not mistake
the goals, ambitions, and dreams of her Communist leaders for the reality with which they have still to grapple.

What, then, should we make of the Great Proletarian

Revolution that has raged across China these past two or three years? According to W. A. C. Adie, in his article on political developments in China, the Cultural Revolution "is really three things in one: an enigmatic multiple power struggle, wrapped in a crusade and superimposed on a scattering of more or less spontaneous, more or less politicized, student riots, strikes, peasant uprisings, mutinies, and palace coups."

Mao's Successor

The first of these three-in-one struggles is the one to which the Western press has devoted the most attention. There was never any doubt about Mao's extraordinary prestige and authority in China, although we have learned now that on several occasions in the past twenty years he has been in a minority in the Communist Party's Central Committee, when it came to policy decisions. Even now it is common ground among almost all Sinologists that whichever faction, or coalition of groups, appears to be the victor in the Peking struggle will inevitably pay lip service to Mao and to Maoism however its own policies may differ from Mao's own.

Probably the easiest way to view the power struggle is as a contest for the succession to Mao, who was seventy-five last year, and whose continued good health seems problematic. It looks now as if there were at least four principal contenders, or four different lobbies, for the succession. One has clearly lost his chance: even if Liu Shao-chi's dismissal and disgrace are not in the end fully ratified, even if the policies and attitudes for which Liu apparently stands are eventually brought back into favor after Mao's last revolt is over, there seems little

political future left for Liu himself. He has been too se-
verely humiliated in the past two years and has forfeited
the respect which a political leader needs, above all in
China. The same goes for his colleagues, Teng Hsiao-ping
and Peng Chen.

The two other contenders are still in the ring, however, in the persons of Lin Piao and Chou En-lai. Lin was
apparently the man favored by Mao himself, at least at
the beginning of the Cultural Revolution. But Lin's skills
are organizational and administrative rather than charismatic, and he seems to have failed to take advantage of
his preferment—perhaps from indifferent health, perhaps
from a sense of inadequacy in not having been able to
rally the Army commanders fully behind the Maoist policies. The surface indications from which alone we are
able to judge this tantalizingly secret power struggle suggest that Lin's star has waned since the brave days of
1966.

Chou's by contrast has gone from strength to strength.
He avoided the trap of openly breaking with Mao, encouraging Mao's radical clique to pull Liu Shao-chi
down. Meanwhile he proved himself indispensable to the
Maoists by keeping the administration going through
all the shocks of internal battle and preventing their
supporters from going so far to the left as to court defeat.
The Prime Minister has emerged tired and haggard from
the demands of the struggle, but with a triple power
base—his own government machine, Hsieh Fu-chih's
Ministry of Public Security organization, and a group of
Army commanders whose loyalty he and Chen Yi, his
best-known Vice-Premier, gained during the guerrilla
days. This begins at last to look impressive by comparison with those of his rivals.

But there is another camp, that of the ultra-Maoists
who have fought for the radical cause throughout the

Cultural Revolution. They do not have a strong candidate for the succession, but they are sufficiently troublesome to damage both Lin's and Chou's claims. Chiang Ching, Mao's wife, is a Johnny-come-lately in the Peking power stakes, and neither Chen Po-ta (Mao's former secretary) nor Kang Sheng, the two senior figures in her salon, are of imperial caliber. But, as John Gittings remarks: "Mao and his small band of radicals could still exercise an influence out of proportion to their apparent political strength."

Power Struggle

The present situation seems to be that these three groups —under Lin Piao, Chou En-lai, and Chiang Ching, respectively—have hammered out the terms of an uneasy coalition. But their own differences are bound to come more into the forefront as their common enemy, Liu Shao-chi, sinks further into political limbo, and as their common master, Mao, eventually retires from the active political scene. Indeed, some of the aspects of the Cultural Revolution which shocked us Westerners most, including the attacks on foreign embassies in Peking in the summer of 1967, were the result of these antagonisms within the pro-Maoist coalition rather than a product of the main struggle between Mao and Liu. There are likely to be more heads to fall before the succession is decided, and the power struggle could last for many more years.

This is only the most superficial aspect of the Cultural Revolution. The leaders are not simply jockeying for power and position; they also have principles and ideals, and the policy aspect of the struggle is probably, in the long run, more important than personalities. The policy

differences between the Mao group and the Liu-ists extend over the whole field, from education to agriculture,
defense to the arts, foreign policy to science.

Perhaps the best way of conveying the essence of the
conflict is to say that it is between optimistic Communists
and pessimistic Communists. It is not quite fair to contrast the Liu-ists as realists and Mao as an idealist. Liu is
still, so far as we know, a convinced Marxist believing
in the ideals of the Communist millennium, while Mao's
policies are not by any means as divorced from reality or
inappropriate to the conditions of rural China today as
some commentators would lead us to believe. Jack Gray
and C. H. G. Oldham demonstrate this in the fields
of economic policy and scientific education. But Mao is
undeterred by the immediate and short-term difficulties
which the Communist program faces in China, whereas
the Liu-ists are daunted by the near-impossibility of
achieving the conversion of 700 million hearts and
minds. Mao is holding out for all or nothing of the Chinese Communist Party's original program, where Liu
would settle for half, consolidating the progress already
achieved and indefinitely postponing the next install-
ments of socialism.

Western observers are tempted to take sides in this
policy debate. Many of them are rooting for Liu because
they regard his policies as being more predictable. They
agree with Mao that Liu-ism is the first step to revisionism
of the kind that we have witnessed in the Soviet Union
and East Europe, differing from him only in welcoming
such a development because it would render China easier
for the West to deal with. But it is obviously short-
sighted and unreal to judge between rival Chinese policies
merely on their consequences in terms of our understanding or interests.

Those who denounce Maoism or support Liu-ism on

the grounds of the relative performance in European societies of communism and capitalism need to be re-
minded how different the Chinese scene is. The Confu-
cianist social organization of China makes Western capitalism and Soviet Communism equally inappropriate,
while her exceptionally low level of material living standards and production techniques pose challenges to her
political leadership which no European or Western government in its prosperous land has ever had to face.

Double Standards

It is against this specific background that Mao's empha-
ses on decentralization, on participatory politics, on self-
reliance, on mass education, on anti-elitism, appear so
attractive. As Gray points out, Western economists concerned with the problems of developing countries have
independently come to recognize in the last few years
that the human, educational, or social factor is a more
important key to economic development than the provision of the purely material inputs of capital equipment
and techniques. Gunnar Myrdal's magnum opus *Asian
Drama* is only the latest plea for this new order of priorities. We are belatedly recognizing the validity of E. F.
Schumacher's concept of "intermediate technology," and
yet we pour scorn on the rural industries of the Chinese Communes. We freely criticize the government of
Indira Gandhi for being too tolerant of the traditional
values and institutions—Brahmanism, caste restrictions,
and Indian disdain for manual labor—which impede economic progress, and yet we also wax indignant over
Mao's refusal to allow schools to be merely places for

book studying. Too often we are guilty of applying double standards to the different methods being used to overcome this, for Westerners, totally unfamiliar problem of getting growth going.

In this special volume from the *Bulletin* we present detailed arguments on both sides for at least one of the important areas of decision-making in China today: the economy. Robert Dernberger gives a careful analysis of the economic problems faced by China—high population growth, shortage of fertile land, limited capacity for savings, and paucity of skills—and concludes that they would be better solved by the "technologists" than by the "radical ideologues" in the leadership. In particular, Dernberger condemns Mao's rejection of material incentives as "bad sociology as well as bad economics." One is tempted to add that the complexity of the current struggle in China may be indicated by the fact that the one man who was all along regarded as the outstanding spokesman of the "technologist" school, Chou En-lai, is currently coordinating the coalition which is supporting Mao, the "radical ideologue."

By contrast, Jack Gray argues the appropriateness of Mao Tse-tung's economic policies for the actual conditions of China. He suggests, in effect, that Liu ism would be the worst of all possible worlds for China, half market economy and half collective, producing lopsided development, aggravating the urbanization problem, and laying the ground work for future rebellions on the part of neglected groups and provinces.

The most serious criticisms of Maoism are twofold. The first concerns the validity of the collectivist solution to the problem of agricultural production and organization. The material incentive in the Chinese Commune is each individual's share of the aggregate profit of the work done by himself and all his colleagues. Is this by definition inadequate? Are there no circumstances in which such incentives would work? Do the Chinese Communes offer in any meaningful way those minimum conditions for successful collectivism? In the present state of our knowledge it would seem foolhardly to offer clear answers to these questions, although what little evidence there is seems enough to provide ammunition to both sides in the debate. I would only add that too few analysts of this problem in its Chinese context make the only really worthwhile comparison, which is with India and the other developing countries of Asia. (Voluntary cooperatives have failed in India.)

The second principal criticism of Mao is surely his sanguine assumption that people will change their ways relatively easily. In order to get the peasants to assert themselves and to seize control of their own environment, Mao has to use human agents who, in the vast majority of the localities to which they are sent with the Maoist message, are only too likely to revert to their basic instincts of autocracy, inequality, bureaucratism, and privilege. Mao Tse-tung seems by inference to have recognized this in his successive recourse to different sets of agents, beginning with the students and younger generation, closely followed by the soldiers and now again by the factory workers. Is there any reason why the latter should succeed any more than the teen-agers or the Army in converting large numbers of people to a new philosophy of life which they themselves do not fully understand—and, if they did, might not fully sympathize with? It is in this sense that Liu's preoccupation with perfecting a nationwide organization which could operate independently of charismatic mystique, and based squarely on the existing human leadership resources, sounds preferable.

The Long Run

The struggle could be described, in Adie's words, as one
between "the revivalist attitude of the dispossessed and
the search of the bureaucrats and the 'new class' for stability." One has to ask: if the Maoist policy is, in the final
resort, doomed to fail because it expects too much of human nature and is insufficiently skeptical of human pro-
fessions, has the entire Cultural Revolution been therefore
a waste of time? What has been gained is a jolt to the
complacency of the bureaucrats, the injection of badly
needed new blood into the organs of local leadership, a
boosting of the morale of the underdogs who still form
such a large part of China even after twenty years of
Communist rule. "The real rebels," as John Gittings puts
it, "were the have-nots of China"—the unemployed students, the contract laborers, the unskilled workers. If
you regard the human factor as the chief bottleneck in
China's development and modernization, then these
gains must appear to outweigh the losses.

But if you regard the material factor as the chief bottleneck, you would find them more than offset by the
waste of several years of formal schooling at all levels, by
the general slowdown in economic activity, by the loss
of foreign exchange earnings, and by the demoralization
of the only body of leadership that had come to grips
with the technical and organizational problems of drag-
ging China belatedly into the twentieth century. Readers will perhaps note the comment of Ray Wylie—who
was at least on the spot when the Cultural Revolution
was being waged—that whereas the students he knew
had not in the past questioned the authority or policies

of the Communist Party, and had precious little understanding of the actual political processes by which their
nation's affairs were governed, their political conscious-
ness was dramatically raised by the Cultural Revolution.

One wonders how permanent this sophistication will
prove, and to what uses it will be put. Mao has already
expressed disappointment over the extent to which the
new freedoms which he has given to the younger generation have been abused and exploited in unconstructive
or anti-social ways. He said the same thing at the time of
the Hundred Flowers Movement more than ten years
ago.

One could summarize the ideological aspect of the Cultural Revolution, therefore, by saying that both the Maoist policy of continuous mystical ferment and the Liu-
ist policy of controlled conventional organization have
their merits: which one is better suited to China's present problems remains unproved, but readers should be
warned against taking things at their face value in China.
On the surface the Maoists have won and the Liu-ists
have lost. But below the surface the victory is not by any
means so clear. Whatever the Peking propaganda organs
may say, the extent to which Maoist policies are actually
being carried out in every province and every county
must remain uncertain. It is hard to imagine that millions
of Party members have become completely silent, inactive, or ideologically subverted after two decades of
continuous power and patronage. Indeed, the whole
question of policy is probably somewhat academic until
the power struggle has been resolved and the identity of
the post-Mao leadership revealed. It might be added that
time is on the side of conservatism, and that where the
power struggle produces a policy vacuum this would
tend to be exploited more by those who think like Liu
than those who think like Mao.

"To rebel is justified." This, the most famous of the slogans informing the Cultural Revolution, is a reminder of the risks of anarchy and administrative breakdown which Mao deliberately courted. Underneath the ideological struggle, underneath the intrigues for the succession to Mao, lies a China full of tensions. There were many forces ready to take advantage of the weakening of centralized Party control from Peking, and much of the strife and violence of the Cultural Revolution was both unintended and ungovernable by the leaders in Peking.

Rivalries between different provinces and regions, between different age groups and interest groups, purely local resentments against local leadership in the Army, in industry, in the cities, in the schools—all these have given the Cultural Revolution its depth, its bitterness, and its confusion. Of all these, it is worth dwelling for a moment on the factor of center-province relations. It may be that we will look back to the pre-Cultural Revolution period in China as the high point of centralized administration. Future generations may wonder why the dream of a politically and economically integrated China should have lasted so long. Many of the Chinese provinces are, after all, as large and populous—even, in speech, as linguistically distinctive—as the great powers of Europe.

It is tempting to exaggerate the consequences of the loosening process which the Cultural Revolution has accelerated. China may never "break down" into separate sovereign states. Indeed the very suggestion that it might betrays an ignorance of the historical differences between China and Europe. But the central government may never again command the same power over the provincial capitals which it enjoyed in the 1950s, and here again India offers the most illuminating comparison. The consequence, of course, would be that development would be uneven among the provinces, and that in-

ternal tensions would become aggravated thereby; the
tendency for the Chinese to be fundamentally preoccupied by their own affairs might also be reinforced. (As a
bonus, the Taiwan question might well prove easier of solution if the Chinese provinces were to become more autonomous.)

It is something of an irony that the Cultural Revolution, with all its tensions and violence (some of which
spilled over into Hong Kong, Cambodia, and other neighboring states) has had the effect of reducing, in the eyes
of those who see it this way, the force of "the Chinese
threat." Last May President Johnson's Under-Secretary
of State Nicholas Katzenbach publicly conceded that
"the military threat posed by Peking can be, and perhaps
at times has been exaggerated." The open internal divisions in a country which for two decades had maintained
an almost uncanny unity in posture toward the outside world naturally made the possibility of aggression
by that country less likely.

The Cultural Revolution has, it is true, injected a
new note of extreme chauvinism in the conduct of
China's relations with a number of foreign countries, including the Soviet Union, North Vietnam, Britain, Burma,
and Nepal. Not since Boxer days have the foreign diplomats in Peking felt closer and more united, whatever the
official differences between their various home governments, in the face of organized hooliganism and public
humiliation of some of their staff. But most of those
same diplomats, judging the matter a little more coolly
now that tempers have calmed down, agree that these
incidents were a natural consequence of the sudden arrival into the charmed circle of Chinese officialdom of
relatively uneducated and untraveled young rebels. The
outside world is to some extent unreal to all Chinese
because of their geographical and historical condition-

ing, but for these new elements who had been left outside the fortresses of power and privilege, foreign countries were even less real.

Cooling Down

Now the excesses of the Red Guards have been tamed and
the conduct of foreign affairs is back in more experienced
and predictable hands. The problem of making the links
between China and the rest of the world both strong
and plain for all Chinese to see is one that will preoccupy
Western, Soviet, and "Third World" diplomats and politicians for another century or more. The Cultural Revolution may in the end prove to have hastened this process
by subjecting a larger sample of the political forces at
work in China to the restraints that actual involvement
in the conduct of foreign policy imposes, and by widening the pathetically limited area of physical relationship and shared experience which the representatives in
China of the outside world enjoy with their hosts.

In practical terms one cannot say that Chinese foreign
policy is yet back to normal. Only one Chinese ambassador is still at his post, the one in Cairo. But it would seem
in the cards that the caution which in the past typified
Chinese foreign policy, in acts if not in words, is likely to
return. Chou En-lai is still in power in Peking, though
with awkward allies who restrict his scope, and the increased influence of the Army in government affairs must
surely have the effect of adding to the voices of restraint.
The colonels at least know the superior hardware which
will confront them if China were to become involved in
direct fighting with either the United States or the Soviet
Union.

It can further be argued that the costly acquisition of
atomic weapons has rendered China more vulnerable to
pre-emptive strikes from those powers who mistrust her
future intentions, and that this alone would add to the
forces of restraint working on Chinese foreign policy.
China's military nuclear and missile program, incidentally,
would appear to have undergone some setbacks during
the most recent phase of the Cultural Revolution.
Michael Yahuda discusses the strategic implications of
this program and suggests that, insofar as it is intended
as a deterrent, it could, because of the consequent need
for bargaining and the communication of intentions, become "the primary agency by which China becomes inducted into fuller participatory membership in the international community of states." You cannot play poker with
a statue.

The prospect of a dying down of the war in Vietnam,
and even of a cease-fire or settlement, adds another dimension to this picture. The Chinese will certainly
maintain their verbal opposition to such a development,
but there is little they can do to stop it if the North Vietnamese and Americans insist, and after a face-saving
period it is not unlikely that the Peking leadership will
come to terms with the new situation in Vietnam. Whatever they may say in public, the Chinese will feel relief
at the withdrawal of the American forces from Vietnam.
Throughout the period of the Cultural Revolution they
have been living on the edge of a volcano in the sense
that escalation of the war to Chinese soil was always a
possibility and always had its advocates in American military circles.

C. P. Fitzgerald suggests that in the long run China
would have to seek a détente either with America or
with the USSR, and he believes that the latter is the more
likely. The Czechoslovakian crisis and the advent of a

Republican administration in Washington must encourage this belief. But this is a most complex speculation, and I do not think we can yet attempt it with any certainty. The kind of chauvinism which leads the Chinese to brandish their fists in all directions at once is still a factor in China's political equation, and if there did have to be a choice between their two big "enemies," some Chinese, especially in the armed forces, might argue that whereas China's western and northern frontiers are disputed by Russia, the Americans do at least accept the eastern and southern borders, which worry the Chinese most.

American hostility to China concerns matters of ideology rather than territorial sovereignty, and the official American position is that Taiwan remains a part of China. The potential conflict of national (as distinct from ideological) interest between the Soviet Union and China is surely greater than that between the United States and China. On the other hand, of course, there is at least a (temporarily underground) pro-Soviet lobby in Peking, and some Chinese leaders might prefer a Soviet to an American *rapprochement* out of pure habit.

There is one more possible factor to be considered here, namely the temptation, so far resisted, for the Soviet leaders to intervene in China on behalf of their friends there. In the light of the situation in East Europe such an intervention must now seem only a remote possibility unless China lapses into another round of civil war and interregional strife.

As Fitzgerald and Richard Harris both observe, the Cultural Revolution has not fundamentally altered China's relations with the outside world. Harris even questions whether China has a foreign policy at all, reminding us in this way that China's conduct of her foreign relations cannot be understood or predicted merely on the basis of the way in which the nation-states of the West, the founders and architects of our present international system, drew up the rules for their own intercourse. This is why Mr. Katzenbach, in the speech already referred to, was wrong in going on to state:

Contact, exchange, detente—all threaten not only the objectives of Peking's foreign policy, but the whole ideological fabric which this generation of leaders has woven together. So long as such attitudes persist in Peking, the establishment of diplomatic relations becomes unrealistic. The underlying premise of such a move—the desire for expanded and improved peaceful contacts between the two countries—appears still to be lacking on the Chinese side.

Delaying Understanding

The mistake here is to assume that the mixture of chauvinism and ideology which dictates China's conduct of her international relations is something capable of being fundamentally changed by any foreseeable set of Chinese leaders in the next decade or decades. If we expect China to respond to our approaches in the way we want, then we are merely courting disappointment. Our choices in the West are two: we can either ignore China and allow this gulf between ourselves and one-quarter of mankind to harden and endure; or else we can try on our side to create conditions more favorable to its ultimate bridging. In neither case can we expect short-term results. The latter policy would involve a search for ways of asserting and advertising the fact that the West respects China, respects Chinese civilization, and respects Chinese territory. To refuse China entry into the United Nations and other international bodies, to refuse to enter into diplomatic relations with her, to maintain the myth that Chiang Kai-shek still governs the Chinese mainland, and to denigrate the Chinese cultural and social tradition is to delay the process of mutual understanding and reconciliation which we ultimately seek.

Let us in honesty recognize that the real stumbling block on the American side is not the overt belligerence of Chinese ideology but the prior commitment to the Nationalists in Taipei. It will not be easy for any American administration to insist on making the subtle but crucial distinction between supporting Chiang Kai-shek's right to rule Taiwan and supporting his hollow pretensions to rule the mainland. We have to learn that friendship becomes exploited if it is taken to mean not merely support and respect and aid but also the encouragement and underwriting of another's impossible dreams and unrealizable ambitions. An honest friend would try to narrow the gap between another's reality and expectation, not widen it.

After Vietnam

As long as American troops have been fighting against Communist insurgents in Vietnam, it has been understandably difficult for the United States to appear to switch its backing from the Chinese Nationalists to the Chinese Communists. But now that this episode is, we hope, almost over, Americans can begin to look at their East Asian relationships more carefully in the light of their real long-term goals. The possibilities of American policies changing anything in East Asia must be acknowledged to be somewhat limited. There is nothing the administration can do, for example, to give China a successful non-Communist régime. But the Chinese are

intelligent and realistic people: to the extent that communism does not work they will in their own good time
quietly abandon it. A far-sighted U.S. policy could plan
for a gradual and tactful disengagement from the Nationalist cause in Taiwan; abandon all restrictions on
trade with and travel in China, unilaterally and without
reciprocity; and commission America's many excellent
and wise Sinologists to advise it in depth and in detail on
how the Chinese government, irrespective of its political
color, could best be induced over the long term to join
the world community in all its activities and concerns.
Only in this way will our children thank us for saving
them from inheriting a world more bitterly divided than
at any time in its history.

THE POLITICAL
STRUGGLE
IN CHINA

For the past three years China has been shaken by a political conflict more violent than anything previously experienced under Communist rule. Because the movement which started it was christened by Mao Tse-tung, its author, as the Great Proletarian Cultural Revolution, we use the short-hand phrase "Cultural Revolution" to denote almost everything that has been going on in China since the later part of 1966. But few outsiders claim to understand what seems to be in part a further installment of the Maoist road to socialism, in part a personal vendetta between Mao and some of his colleagues (or between rivals for the Maoist succession), in part a revolt of the provinces and regions against tight central control from Peking, in part a reshuffle of power in favor of the Army at the expense of the Communist Party.

In the first article that follows, W. A. C. Adie outlines the chief stages of the Cultural Revolution, the main theories that have been advanced about its origins and its significance, and the principal consequences that would seem to flow from it. In the second article, John Gittings discusses the most recent developments of the past twelve months or so in an attempt to depict the situation that now exists in Chinese politics. Finally, Ray Wylie, who was teaching in China during the Cultural Revolution, gives a first-hand impression of what it was like and what it seemed to be about.

China's "Second Liberation" in Perspective

W. A. C. Adie

Peking says that its Great Proletarian Cultural Revolution "will inevitably set ablaze all parts of the world." Back in 1961, it had already proclaimed that "Paris Communes will surely cover the world."

But Peking's words, often rendered outlandish by literal translation, must not be taken at face value, unless the "face" is Chinese. In order to understand the real significance of the Cultural Revolution for the outside world, a non-Chinese must attempt a mental emigration into a universe of profoundly alien political traditions and ways of speech and action. The closer any account of Chinese politics gets to the truth, the more irritatingly paradoxical and mystifying it must become. One cause of the present confusion in China is that traditional double-talk and opportunism, codified into the Maoist jargon all have been forced to learn, created a semantic fog in which even the Chinese did not know whose side they were on, who was winning, which way to switch, or when. The flood carried them along. Some tried to dam it, others to swim on it, with the intention of doing the opposite when expedient.

Mao claims that he loosed the flood, but did not fore-

see the result. Though one of his aims was to cure some
of the Chinese habits he found undesirable, such as
avoidance of open conflict or discussion, deviousness,
and fatalism or mock submissiveness in the face of authority, the present effect of the Cultural Revolution has
been to double the premium on Orwellian duckspeak
and cynical all-way reinsurance. However, the notion has
been put over that the "masses" can actually change
their rulers, instead of cheating them with passive resistance. For Mao, the truths of Marxism can be summed
up in the phrase: to rebel is justified. Actually it was Mencius who taught that rebellion against a decadent
dynasty was justified by its success; Mao's revision of
Mencius, while at the moment excluding periodical elections as a less destructive substitute for the recurrent revolutions of the dynastic cycle, seeks to achieve the effect of a permanent plebiscite, a continuous rebellion,
rolling the wheel of history steadily on.

Was the Cultural Revolution the second liberation of
China, as the Chinese say? Was it an ideological crusade
or a struggle for power for the succession? In order to
answer such questions we must look briefly at some of
the earlier history of Mao and his movement.

Of the two main schools of thought on these issues,
one casts Mao, or the Maoist Messianism, as prime
mover; the other looks for objective causes, either impersonal factors such as internal socioeconomic development
and foreign policy setbacks, or old personal feuds and
new clashes of interest between functional groups. While
most foreign scholars concentrate on the impersonal,
Chinese sources both on and off the mainland stress the
personal and conspiratorial. Even the *cherchez la femme*
school is well represented, the woman in question being
Mme. Mao, Chiang Ching.

Among those who hold Mao responsible are found

both his most earnest supporters and critics, fallaciously supposing that what actually happened was largely as Mao intended. Some consider the Cultural Revolution a sublime experiment in social engineering, a necessary antidote to the bureaucratic degeneration and dehumanization of industrializing states—socialist or otherwise—and some, like the Soviet Communists, denounce the whole enterprise as an attack on the genuine Marxist-Leninists of China, motivated by petit bourgeois fanaticism and chauvinistic war mania.

Allowing for the wide differences of standpoint and value judgments, these observers are generally agreed that Mao and his close collaborators purposely provoked the Cultural Revolution in order to divert China's revolution from the path of Soviet-style Communism and keep it moving toward a new form of social organization. Some Chinese spokesmen, including Mao himself, support this view, suggesting that Mao had found an antidote to Stalinism. For example, in an interview with a Uruguayan, Foreign Minister Marshal Chen Yi said:

At the Twentieth Party Congress Khrushchev said that Stalin had killed many people. That's not important. That he had stimulated the cult of personality. That's secondary. Maybe Stalin made these mistakes. But there was a more serious one. By stimulating industry and technology [that is, urban work and the intellectuals] without resolving the agricultural problem, he contributed to the process of degeneration.

He did not take steps to eliminate the capitalist evils of intellectuality. He was too impatient to declare there was no longer a class struggle in Russia. . . . afterwards Khrushchev used the intellectuals to restore capitalism. And imperialism spurred him on. . . . we are attempting to eliminate the intellectual class.

Mao himself said something to the effect that when building such a great Communist party he had never expected to have to destroy it again. Sometimes the Cultural Revolution was described as a preparation for war. However, Mao's politico-military technique—what he calls the algebra of revolution—has always shown a marked tendency to "change the signs" of negative phenomena and turn them to his advantage by introducing some new element into the equation. Much of Mao's famous "thought" is really a codification of opportunism, a rationalization of improvisations imposed by past situations. The evidence suggests that in the Cultural Revolution too Mao was not whipping up a paper tiger but trying to manipulate a number of real and serious "contradictions," as he would call them, so that they would cancel each other out.

Dissensions and Contradictions

What were these contradictions? Perhaps the most important is the one between Mao's thought, a source of legitimacy but closely linked with practical policy, and the changing reality of a modernizing China. Briefly, the characteristics which made Mao's thought an integrative force while China was disintegrated under the rule of foreign invaders and war lords contained in itself the seeds of disintegration once Mao and his New Model Army became the government. This contradiction could be obscured while Mao was content to reign rather than rule. But when he—or others acting in his name—tried to reassert direct personal control from Peking the split between the ideological and organizational leaderships of the Party was bound to become evident.

In more concrete terms, there were longstanding dissensions between groups in the Party whose experience

lay mainly in rural guerrilla warfare on the one side
and underground agitation among urban workers, students, and intellectuals on the other. Consequently, differing group loyalties and policies on a series of problems
emerged after the liberation. Naturally enough these
problems revolved around the key issues of unification
and defense: through what apparatus or ideology to
achieve the right balance of centralization or decentralization, how far to rely on Soviet methods or help in
modernizing national defense, and so on.

Chinese sources say that there were many struggles
and three "inner revolutions" in the Party against "erroneous lines," especially the "bourgeois military line"
which stressed training and equipment rather than morale and Mao's thought. In fact the issues were far more
complicated, and a given group, such as Party officials at
provincial level, could play a Maoist or anti-Maoist role
at different places and different times, while always pro-
fessing loyalty to the Party line.

One of the revelations of the Cultural Revolution is that
Mao had not really achieved a high degree of central
control in China at all. Perhaps the size and diversity of
the country and of its population made it impossible. It
also appears that the successes as well as the failures of
his régime had created economic and social polarization
and tensions which were bound in any case to break out
in the sort of "Hungarian incidents" that actually did
occur, though with Mao's blessing. Some of the conflicts
between what are now called "Mao's line" and "the
erroneous line" ascribed to President Liu were about the
right way to exploit and solve these tensions—in Mao's
language, "contradictions." Basically, the question was
whether to dam the pent-up frustrations of discontented
students, unskilled workers, and other left-out groups by
palliative measures and repression, or loose the flood and

use it to power a new revolutionary upsurge, while Mao
swam strongly with the current.

Thus, it can be argued that the Cultural Revolution is
really three things in one: an enigmatic multiple power
struggle, wrapped in a crusade, and superimposed on a
scattering of more or less spontaneous, more or less politicized student riots, strikes, peasant uprisings, mutinies,
and palace coups. The main personalities involved have
apparently been President Liu, Premier Chou, and Defense Minister Marshal Lin—the three active vice-chair-
men of the Central Committee of the Party—and one or
two other possible successors to Mao. In general, however, the struggle has been carried on by proxy, with a
mysterious "black backer" sponsoring attacks on subordinates of his opponent. The crusade element is quite genuine, but the details were improvised to a large extent,
despite brave talk of "Chairman Mao's great strategic
plan." The escalation of U.S. troop strength in Vietnam
and other foreign events played an unmeasurable part in
modifying what plans Mao may have had.

Mao's Algebra

The transformation of Maoism from an integrative into a
disintegrative formula may be largely explained first by
the institutionalization of what was initially a revivalist,
almost religious nationalist and social movement, and
secondly by a change in the dimensions of the problem
to which the algebra, or rather alchemy, was applied.

Mao's aim, like that of previous Chinese reformers and
revolutionaries, was the "self-strengthening" of China and
the Chinese, who individually and as a group felt pow-
erless and humiliated after the Opium Wars. According to

Chinese traditional thought, this weakness and disorder was the sign of degeneration of the dynasty. The mandarins tried to strengthen it from above by adopting Western techniques; the Boxer rebels tried to regenerate China by a mass movement from below; foreign-educated Dr. Sun Yat-sen, the father of the Chinese Revolution, brought in foreign political ideas but had no troops; the first President of the Republic, Yuan Shih-kai, had the modern troops but no ideas. Sun Yat-sen recognized that the Chinese people were "a sheet of sand" and sought their "cement" in bourgeois nationalism. Having indoctrinated the youth with nationalism, Chiang Kai-shek's regime found itself forced by public opinion into a conflict with Japan in conditions which eventually enabled Mao's Communists to emerge as victors.

From his experience as a guerrilla leader, Mao devised a set of tactics for cementing his mass movement, combining those of his predecessors, which were perfected and imposed on it in laboratory conditions at the guerrilla base in remote Yenan. While Stalin had relied on Byzantine intrigue and ruthless police methods, Mao sought the *Gleichschaltung* of "hearts and minds" by techniques analogous to religious conversion, developed from the methods used to win over captured enemy soldiers. Crudely speaking, the method applies a psychological solvent before the cement, both stages being necessary for complete "rectification." It aims, like Confucianism, at a spontaneous self-discipline, but it relies not on the cool "self-cultivation" of a library Communist but on the elemental power of mass hysteria and group pressure. As Mao says, to treat the disease and save the patient, first we have to shake the patient up by struggle —a reign of terror of some sort, or a war—and make him realize he is ill; then we maneuver him into a position where he will switch sides or pretend that he was on

"our" side all the time; once committed, he will talk, then
think, "correctly." "They" are all patients—unpeople or
ghosts—but can be converted into "people" once awak-
ened by struggle. When outnumbered, we temporarily
have some of the unpeople join us in order to beat them
without fighting. One way is by embroiling them with a
more powerful third party which we use to force them
toward us under the shock treatment of war or emergency. Thus their sign changes from negative to positive, and we always have a majority on "our" side. While
promoting the united front by armed struggle we also
build up an ideologically pure party to make sure the
process is irreversible.

From 1942 onward, supporters of Soviet-trained or
Soviet-influenced Communists such as Wang Ming were
thus "remolded." Although the technique had worked on
people who felt dispossessed and insecure, and in the
siege conditions of Yenan, when Mao moved to Peking
and tried to apply it to the entire Chinese people, his
spell was broken. Confucius, it has been said, wanted
gentlemen but he got players. In time, Mao's Chinese also
learned to go through the motions at the constant
sessions of "Criticism and Self-Criticism," without really
changing their minds. The conditions of stress receded,
and after the liberation in 1949, Soviet-influenced Communists tried to develop Mao's doctrine from Utopia to
science. Indeed, even before the liberation two distinct
theories of the Party's role had openly emerged in the
writings of Chairman Mao and of Liu Shao-chi. In Mao's
thought (especially as revised for the purposes of the
Cultural Revolution by Marshal Lin or whoever stood
behind him) the Party was regarded essentially as a mass
movement, a mere assemblage of like-minded people in
a personal if not mystic relationship with their leader
which ensures that they all move as one. But for Liu, it

was its organizational structure which gave the Party its fighting strength.

This emphasis on organization is linked to appreciation of the importance of technology. Liu wrote in 1947: "When we build a new China . . . today's military commanders themselves will go to the factories to work. At that time, technical work will decide everything." Mao on the other hand always held that "men not weapons decide the issue of war" and sought to apply this tenet to peacetime construction also.

The "Two Lines" in Practice

This ideological split between the revivalist attitude of the dispossessed and the search of the bureaucrats and the "new class" for stability found expression in complex struggles and policy changes from 1949 onward. Generally speaking, the Maoist line emphasized stirring up the initiative of the lowest levels of the Party and of society by mass movements on the analogy of a human wave attack, but the Party constantly emphasized the manipulation of these movements by its apparatus from above. By mid-1961, the Party had some seventeen million members, but only 3.4 million of them had joined before 1949. Many of the old cadres were reluctant to give full rein to the grass-roots activists in the countryside, some of whom had a deplorably low "ideological level." Thus the Party line oscillated between periods of "mass movement" and of bureaucratic control.

Another major problem was that of vertical versus horizontal control and the relative independence of the government, Army, and Party power structures. To begin with, the country was under decentralized military control, and some leaders regarded the Party as merely an emanation of the Army. The first purges and centralization measures occurred in the context of the Korean War. After Stalin's death an "anti-Party group" controlling the key industrial areas of Manchuria and Shanghai-Nanking was removed and a number of local potentates called to work in Peking, though others remained entrenched in their fiefs, such as Sinkiang, Outer Mongolia, and Central-South China. After this, Liu Shao-chi controlled the Party apparatus, the trade unions, and the Youth League, while Chou En-lai had the government machine. Secretary-General Teng Hsiao-ping, who had led the attack on the "anti-Party group" at a Party conference in March 1955, was shortly afterward elevated to the Politburo of the Party, as was Marshal Lin Piao, probably because the other two Marshals, Chu Teh and Peng Te-huai, had compromised themselves.

In his report on the revision of the constitution of the Communist Party of China at the Eighth Congress in 1956, Secretary-General Teng announced the setting up of "additional central organs in the Central Committee owing to the pressure of Party work." In effect this meant a substantial delegation of political power by Mao Tse-tung to Liu (as the senior vice-chairman of the newly established Standing Committee of the Politburo) and to Teng (as head of the secretariat in charge of the daily work of the Central Committee). Teng and Liu were in the first line while Mao went back to the second line. However, Mao interpreted the outbreak of minor "Hungarian incidents" in 1956 as a signal that the Party bureaucracy needed "rectification" by the public. In 1957, the students of Peking University played a leading part in this movement, putting up large character posters criticizing the "Party empire." But these "hundred flowers" soon wilted under a counterattack by the Party apparatus, reportedly led by Liu Shao-chi, Peking's Mayor Peng and other hard liners. The senior critics, mostly non-Party administrators and intellectuals, were purged as "rightists." The net result of the movement was that Party officials and committees took over more economic management in addition to political administration, reducing the role of Chou En-lai's government apparatus throughout the country. Thus a tendency to establish vertical control from Peking through the government machine and its local branches, and in mass organizations such as the trade unions, was reversed in favor of increased control of local matters by the local Party committees.

In May 1958, a special second session of the 1956 Congress was held to consecrate a more activist Party line in both internal and external affairs. This was involved with the decision to reject certain Soviet proposals on joint defense and nuclear weapons, and the defeat of the "erroneous military line" which had appeared after the Korean War—namely, the imitation of, and hence dependence on, the USSR, "under the signboard of regularization and modernization." (This viewpoint had its counterpart in industrial policy, education, and so on, in the "purely productional, purely professional viewpoint.") The 1958 crisis saw the election of Marshal Lin as vice-chairman of the Central Committee, while Marshal Peng, figurehead of the professionals, was "rectified" at a subsequent session of the Military Commission of the Central Committee. The Communes and militia must be seen as part of an alternative defense plan, associated with Lin Piao and reliance on Soviet aid and methods.

According to the resolution of November 1958, the Communes were also to combine industry, agriculture, trade, education, and military affairs, and to integrate government administration with their own management.

This would "gradually lessen and finally eliminate" not only the differences between town and country, worker and peasant, and mental and manual labor, but even *the internal function of the state."* In reality, however, the abandonment of the Soviet model of industrialization and the decentralization of economic initiative under theoretically centralizing Party control—the "great leap forward"—led to even more empire building, this time by local Party bosses, and confusion reigned. Treating Mao, as he later said, like an ancestor at his funeral, the Party deified but disobeyed him.

In 1959, Marshal Peng led the professionals in an attempt to reverse Mao's policies, allegedly in collusion with Khrushchev. At a stormy plenum of the Central Committee Mao is said to have threatened to go out and raise another peasant army to fight his own Party which had become another corrupt Kuomintang.

Whether this is true or not, something like it actually happened, starting immediately with the replacement of Peng by Marshal Lin as Defense Minister. In 1960, Lin launched a campaign ostensibly for "study of the thoughts of Mao Tse-tung" in the Army, linked with the publication of the fourth volume of Mao's works, dealing with his defeat of the Kuomintang in which the countryside surrounded the cities.

Poster Campaigns

In the Army's study material (later notorious in the form of the "little red book") Maoism was given a new slant and the charisma of the man was used to confer a talismanic quality on the works, selected and annotated under Lin Piao's aegis. At the same time, however, great emphasis was placed inside the Party apparatus on the strengthening of organization and discipline following the elevation of the former secret police chief, Lo Jui-ching, to the position of Army chief of staff. The Party's legal, judicial, and public security organs extended their power and in some localities (as interrogation of escapees has shown) everything was in fact run by a few Party members who held office in these organizations.

On the other hand, in some provinces at least a movement to recreate the rural base of the Party had also been in progress since the 1959 plenum. As in Mao's guerrilla days, associations of poor peasants were formed and mass struggle meetings and poster campaigns against bureaucratic Party officials were held to "form a new kernel of Party leadership and a new industrial and agricultural revolutionary army, to lay the foundations of a new type of village and a new type of city." Meanwhile, the economic dislocation resulting from the excesses of the "great leap forward" of 1958 and the series of natural disasters had obliged the Party's "first line" to make concessions to the "spontaneous capitalistic tendencies" of the peasantry, and give material incentives to the workers. This led to renewed polarization and demoralized some Party workers.

Taking this as evidence that Marshal Peng had been right in his attack on Mao in 1959, a number of intellectuals both in and out of the Party propaganda apparatus published allegorical writings calling in veiled terms for his rehabilitation and denouncing Mao's line. At the end of December, their "backer," Mayor Peng of Peking, held a secret conference to collect evidence of mistakes in the 1958 policy in the hope of "allowing Chairman Mao to calm down and examine himself," as one participant allegedly put it. Another, however, pointed out that "in the history of the Party no mistakes of line have been corrected by those who made them." Hence this group took no overt action.

Open Criticism

At an enlarged Central Committee Work Conference held a month later in January 1962, President Liu openly criticized a number of Mao Tse-tung's policies. While Mao Tse-tung and Marshal Lin Piao maintained that "the situation is very favorable, but there are still many problems," Liu, Teng, and the other first-line leaders thought that "the very favorable situation the Chairman has discussed refers to the political situation. But the economic situation cannot be said to be very favorable; it is very unfavorable." Liu described China's economy as "on the brink of collapse," China's financial difficulties as "grave." The losses in agriculture alone, he said, would require seven or eight years to repair. The crisis was seventy per cent the result of man-made disasters. Unwillingness to admit our difficulties, he said, is definitely not the bearing of a revolutionary or a proper Leninist attitude. He also called for rehabilitation of a number of Party officials and technical specialists who had spoken up against Mao's great leap forward in 1959, though he did not seek to "reverse the verdict" on Marshal Peng because the latter had "maintained illicit relations with foreign countries."

After this meeting, Mao decided to correct these "erroneous tendencies" by reclaiming the powers which he had delegated in 1956 to Liu and Teng. At the Tenth Plenum of the Eighth Central Committee held in September 1962, he abolished the second line. As he revealed later in a speech on October 25, 1966, in the last decade what he called "a considerable number of independent kingdoms" had grown up, the most important of which was of course the Party apparatus controlled by Liu and Teng. As Mao put it, "a bourgeois headquarters had entrenched itself in the apparatus of the dictatorship of the proletariat." In order to deal with this high-level opposition within the Party, Mao reverted to his usual strategy of promoting a mass movement and class struggle from below, to secure a majority.

After the Tenth Plenum what was called a "socialist education movement" was generalized in the rural areas, in which the peasants and officials were to "rectify" each other. But the officials either did not believe in, or did not approve of, the supposedly revolutionary tendencies of the poorer peasants; the movement was bogged down and distorted. Opinions in the Party differed on who was to blame. In the early 1960s, blame for the mistakes in the "great leap" of 1958 had been laid on the basic-level cadres rather than on those of the middle level.

But by now it was the provincial authorities who were setting up "private kingdoms." So a ten-point instruction attributed to Mao said in May 1963 that ninety-five per cent of the basic-level cadres were good or pretty good. They were to hold ideological study and struggle sessions and so purify first themselves and then the poor and lower-middle peasants, with whom they were to form an alliance in the course of village class warfare. In the process, new peasant associations were to be formed so that the basic-level units would be controlled not from above, by Party organs, but from below, by the masses themselves. The resultant upsurge in revolutionary enthusiasm would carry the revolution on, as it should have done in 1958.

The Central Committee soon issued a further ten points which stressed material incentive, and warned against victimizing rich—productive—peasants. In June 1964, another order put the peasants' associations under control of the district Party committees. In January 1965, the Maoist line came back with the "Twenty-Three Articles," foreshadowing the "Sixteen Points" issued in August 1966 by the Eleventh Plenum, which ratified Mao's version of the Cultural Revolution. It proclaimed class struggle and the supervisory role of the poorer peasants, stating for the first time that "persons in authority taking the capitalist road" existed at all levels in the Party, specifically including the top. Still nothing much came out of the countryside. This time the revolution had to take place in the urban centers, beginning, symbolically, with Peking University, and soon engulfing most cities with strikes, riots, and peasant *jacquaeries*. Meanwhile Lin Piao's drive to restore the primacy of his version of Mao's thought in the Army had begun to extend into civilian life, against the increasingly overt resistance of organizations concerned with industry, trade union affairs, youth, and education, expressed in the relevant press organs.

Launched in 1963, the campaign for the "whole country to emulate the army" in studying Mao's thought had developed into cover for a system in which "political organs" largely staffed by transferred soldiers were being set up in key civilian organizations. Being responsible to the Military Commission, they by-passed Teng's Party Secretariat. Military figures also took over many important posts such as the Ministry of Machine Building concerned with nuclear weapons. Gradually the "study and labor" line of the Army paper—that factories should be schools of Mao's thought, and schools should be factories —came out on top.

On March 11, Lin symbolically addressed a letter of commendation to certain industrial enterprises for "putting politics on the forefront" in the work of management. In June, the Army newspaper spelled out the message with an article about a certain plant which had since 1961

"carried out in earnest instructions of the Military Commission of the Central Committee of the CCP and Comrade Lin Piao in placing the living study and application
of Chairman Mao's thought in first place." Some people,
said the article, "say that the job of factories is production
and their foremost task should be the turning out of products; and how can it be the fostering of revolutionized
people? We say: this is wrong. . . . How are [our fac-
tories] different from capitalist factories if their sole purpose is to turn out products?"

The Cultural Revolution has produced much evidence
about the grievances of workers, peasants, and students
which complicated the issue. A poster seen in Shanghai in
January 1967 listed thirty-five grievances of the peasantry,
complaining that the countryside was used as the rubbish
bin of the towns ("no matter what the crime, anyone in
need of remolding is sent out to the country, some for reform through labor"), then listing many ways in which
"the dogs of officials" and city workers are better off than
the peasants, discriminate against and exploit them, de-
priving them of democracy and economic independence.
Red Guard newspapers have also referred to the iniqui-
tous conditions of work under the "contract and temporary work system" in industry (now blamed on Liu Shao-
chi).

January Revolution

The material incentives system had not only exacer-
bated social tensions, but increased economic pressures
such as demand for consumer goods, which did not suit
Mao's ideas either of "building socialism" or making China
the arsenal of the world revolution. All these tensions

erupted in the "January Revolution," once the first stage of the Cultural Revolution had reduced the local Party and police bosses to "paper tigers." The Communist Party and security authorities brought to bear the usual repressive measures—both police spying and pressure and mass "struggle" meetings—against the first stirrings of revolt, but they suddenly found themselves denounced for carrying out a "white terror." Even Mao's study was allegedly bugged by the security men.

The real crunch of the Cultural Revolution came at the turn of the year 1966-67, culminating with the abortive attempt to set up "Paris Communes" in Shanghai and Peking after "seizure of power" from the legal authorities by self-styled proletarian revolutionaries. It is impossible to analyze here the complexities of these events. The important point is that this revolutionary movement "from below," initially encouraged by Mao and his wife and leaders close to them, was blocked, apparently with Mao's assent, in such a way that power eventually fell into the hands of the military commanders and of Chou En-lai's government machine, led by his Vice-Premiers, especially Hsieh Fu-chih, Minister of Public Security.

Subsequently three rival hierarchies have coexisted, employing against each other the classic Maoist "united front" techniques of simultaneous "unity and struggle," and "Let's you and him fight" while maintaining leverage through recognition of Mao's "latest directives," interpreted in their own way. These "three kingdoms" have been the Army under Lin Piao's Military Committee of the Communist Party Central Committee; the dwindling Cultural Revolution Group under Chen Po-ta and Chiang Ching, loosely controlling some Red Guard and Red Rebel groups; and the government machine under Chou En-lai's State Council.

Broadly speaking, the period up to September 1967

was one in which the scattered exponents of law and order tried to cope with the fallout of the January Revolution, with very uneven success. Since then the revolutionary forces have been fighting a rear-guard action as the
new organs of State power—the three-way Revolutionary
Committees—have been set up "from above" under the
hegemony of military commanders and rehabilitated
Party officials, with "rebels" in the minority. This process was uneven, owing to such incidents as a resurgence
of Chiang Ching, purge of military leaders, and renewed
denunciations of propagandists in March 1968, repeating
the pattern of the previous spring. But by September
1968, Revolutionary Committees had been imposed on
all twenty-nine provinces, "autonomous areas," and major
cities, often by flagrant compromise with hitherto "anti-
Maoist" leaders and organizations. In the small hours of
July 28, Mao had received Red Guard leaders and tear-
fully intimated that they had betrayed his trust. The ban-
ner of the Cultural Revolution was now to be held up by
the industrial workers "under leadership" of the Army.

What Went Wrong?

Industrial and railway workers had played a major part
in the "January Revolution" and its aftermath. What went
wrong with the "Commune" idea at that time? Why should
it go better now?

In its first phase the Cultural Revolution was apparently confined to educational and research institutions
and to the cultural and propaganda apparatus of the Party,
with which Mao had expressed dissatisfaction several
times in previous years. It was not until May 1966 that

the campaign was given clear political significance by press attacks on the Peking Party Committee, in the person of the editor of its newspaper.

Since the great student movement of May 4, 1919, the Chinese have thought that a political revolution needs a cultural revolution first, to prepare public opinion. Mayor Peng of Peking had tried to keep things on the level of an academic debate, but on May 25 seven philosophy teachers at Peking University, led by Nieh Yuan-tzu, symbolically put up a poster criticizing the principal and others. They were universally condemned as anti-Party elements, but on June 1, 1966, Mao hailed Nieh's poster as the harbinger of a Peking Commune, like the Paris one of 1871, and had it put in the *People's Daily.* Everybody immediately sided with Nieh and denounced the principal. Spontaneity? Though she belonged to Mme. Mao's "salon group," Nieh could hardly have acted without assurances from an important backer.

Some evidence for the beginning of the Red Guards goes back to March. According to foreign eyewitnesses, before Mao had openly legitimized their action, disgruntled students had in several cities begun to riot against academic, then Party, authorities. Other evidence suggests that these minority groups were put up to it by students recently seconded from the Army, or by Security agents, probably *provocateurs.* After the arrival in the colleges of work teams sent by the "anti-Maoist" group running the "Socialist Cultural Revolution," no more was heard of "Communes"; soon, however, the teams clashed with the students, some of whom may have known about Mao's circular of May 16 denouncing Mayor Peng's sabotage of the Cultural Revolution, starting a new group and renaming it the "great *proletarian* Cultural Revolution."

On Army Day (August 1), an "enlarged" session of the Party Central Committee opened, not attended by several important leaders and intimidated, according to some reports, by Maoist supporters such as were soon to emerge as Red Guards. It issued "sixteen points" directing that the Cultural Revolution was to be run from below against the "capitalist roaders," that is, against opponents of the ultra-Maoist line of the new Cultural Revolution Group, in which Mao's wife and his secretary Chen Po-ta (editor of the theoretical journal *Red Flag*) played a prominent role. However, the campaign was not to interfere with industrial or agricultural production or the work of scientists and technicians, and there was to be no outside interference in the Army.

After this partial ratification of the ultra-revolutionary line, the Red Guards' Boxer-type "reign of terror" was supposed to prepare for the transformation of China's factories, rural peoples' Communes, schools, training enterprises, service trades, and Party and government organizations into "great and truly revolutionary schools like the PLA." Whether under orders or not, Red Guards who roamed the country attacking local "capitalist roaders" did get involved with workers and peasants, often meeting violent opposition.

In November, Mme. Mao leapt to prominence as sponsor of a "new stage of the Cultural Revolution." She made a keynote speech and a number of cultural organizations were incorporated into the Army, to which she was appointed adviser on cultural affairs. This signified either an attempt to head off, or ratification of, a move to abandon the limitations set for the Cultural Revolution in August. In any case, next day Red Guards directed by associates of Mme. Mao attacked newspaper offices in Shanghai in preparation for the overthrow of the local Party machine and establishment of a "Paris Commune." The ensuing disorders were matched in many other parts of the country. The extension of the Cultural Revolution to

production units was announced on December 26, Mao's
birthday, and he sanctioned the Army's intervention on
January 21. Both moves were partly a recognition of *faits
accomplis.*

Instead of powering a political revolution against the
bureaucracy, the frustrations of many people had been
released in the form of demands for better pay and conditions. Bowing to these demands, local bosses sent train-
loads of workers to riot in Peking—in answer to the Red
Guards Peking had sent to them. The Maoists had to divert this trend of "counter-revolutionary economism"
back against the "capitalist roaders" by organizing adult
"revolutionary rebels" among suitable sections of the
labor force, with support from the Army. As anarchy
spread, both the police and the mutual surveillance system crumbled. Mobs attacked Party and police offices
where the incriminating dossiers were kept, but the officials resorted to the Army as an "air raid shelter" for themselves and their records.

In Peking itself, the Red Guards attacked many senior
government and military leaders and the propaganda apparatus was purged anew. Its new chief, Tao Chu, disap-
peared into dissidence. Mme. Mao demanded that the
Public Security be taken over by the Army. In one day
several Red Guard groups occupied the Ministry. These
attacks indirectly threatened both Chou En-lai and Lin
Piao via close subordinates, but soon Mme. Mao had to
appear in public with Chou and draw the line between a
number of "capitalist roaders" who had been dragged
before Red Guard kangaroo courts and a group of Minis-
ters and officers whom she now admitted to be good students of Chairman Mao after all, notably Security Minister Hsieh Fu-chih.

Peking never recognized the establishment of Shanghai's Commune on February 5. Chou and other leaders

declared that the time was not ripe for introduction of direct proletarian democracy by elections. Mao said that the change of state system would involve recognition by foreign governments. He sent back the "rebel" leaders to Shanghai with new instructions: the line was not now for seizure of power by a "Great Alliance" of the more or less spontaneous "rebel" organizations, each with their sectional interest or loyalties, but by a triple alliance of "rebels" with rehabilitated Party cadres and the military, with the latter clearly in control.

Thus the stage was set for the "February adverse current" in which many of the effects of the Red Guard terror were negated and the bureaucracy settled back into the old mold. "Hoodwinked" by economism, the masses had failed Mao, and the country was back to the situation of 1949, as Chou said—under semi-independent military rule. This being so, it was logical that the "leftists" in the Cultural Revolution Group—Mme. Mao, her cronies, and perhaps a "big backer"—should sponsor the slogan, "Drag out the handful of 'capitalist roaders' in the Army." This led, however, to fighting in almost every military area, notably to the mutiny in Wuhan, quelled by paratroops and gunboats. Sent to cope, Premier Chou's Vice-Premier Hsieh Fu-chih and a "leftist," Wang Li, were at one point arrested by the local commander. This ominous event, followed by a tour of disturbed provinces by Mao himself, induced the Cultural Revolution Group to change its line again, especially as the "leftists" had also gone too far in their indirect attacks on Chou En-lai's civilian power base, with serious repercussions on the economy and foreign relations. Though space does not allow a full discussion, it may be argued that the siege of the Soviet and other embassies and the aberrations of foreign policy in mid-1967 were essentially functions of a power struggle within the Cultural Revolution Group.

International Factors

The foreign policy aspects of the Cultural Revolution are dealt with elsewhere in this issue, but this is a convenient place to touch on two points where they affected internal developments. At the outset, events in Vietnam and other Chinese plans for South Asia played an important but uncertain role, as did the theories propagated, perhaps believed, by Mao and others that an American-Formosan attack, a joint Soviet-American attack, or a Soviet-American war was imminent. It is known that decisive moves were made by Mao to launch the Cultural Revolution on the same day that representatives of the Japanese Communist Party met Mao (with Teng Hsiao-ping, Kang Sheng, and Tao Chu) outside Canton on March 28, 1966.

The Japanese, who also visited Pyongyang and Hanoi on this trip, reportedly advocated "united action" with the USSR over Vietnam. They had agreed on a communiqué with Chou En-lai, Teng Hsiao-ping, Peng Chen, and others but Mao cancelled it, shouting "You weak-kneed people in Peking!" Mao also issued orders to have Peng's February program for the Cultural Revolution "criticized," and to dissolve the Party Central Propaganda Department, the Party Peking Committee, and the five-man Cultural Revolution Group (led by Peng Chen).

"United action" had evidently been favored by Chief of Staff Lo Jui-ching, judging by some of his writings in 1965, and allegedly also by Liu Shao-chi, who was at that moment in Pakistan. On his way back he allegedly plotted against Mao in Sinkiang with the local satrap, Wang En-mao. Like other rulers of areas with a large non-Chinese population, such as Tibet, Yunnan, and Inner Mongolia, Wang resisted extension of the Cultural Revolution to his fief, presumably in order to avoid new anti-Chinese unrest. Similarly, other leaders from the Moslem areas had long been associated with the policy of relations "in the Bandung spirit" with Indonesia, Pakistan, Burma, etc. This was denounced in 1967 as a traitorous policy of Liu Shao-chi.

It was later alleged that Peng Chen had used the war scare as a cover for anti-Mao coup preparations early in 1966. Actually the scare in the Chinese press was at its height in late 1965, when Mao told Edgar Snow he did not expect a war, whereas in March 1966 he told the Japanese it was inevitable. In the interim, there had been the debacle in Indonesia, the fall of Nkrumah, etc., and the "Bandung" policy lay in ruins.

During the summer of 1967, Foreign Minister Marshal Chen Yi, Liao Cheng-chih, and the foreign relations and trade organizations generally were subjected to "struggle" by Red Guards and "rebels," masterminded by some members of the Cultural Revolution Group. They denounced Chen for following Liu's policy of pandering to Ne Win and Sukarno and failing to protect the overseas Chinese in their countries. In self-defense the Foreign Ministry and related organizations were forced to adopt to some extent the style of "Boxer diplomacy" which was carried to extremes by its enemies, with the apparent aim of provoking foreign retaliation. Chou En-lai later said the "ultra-leftists" had done irreparable damage to China's foreign relations. Relations with Burma and Indonesia, both visited by Liu Shao-chi, were ruined. There is circumstantial evidence that certain people in China had some foreknowledge of the "Gestapu" coup planned in Indonesia for October 1, 1965—China's National Day— the success of which would have had repercussions on

Vietnam. The abortive "Second Bandung" at Algiers was also expected to help solve the Vietnam problem.

The relationship between the "erroneous military line" followed (according to Peking) by Hanoi's southbound forces in 1964-65 and the Maoists' struggle against the similar line in their own military and foreign policy is too complex to go into here. Suffice it to say that in Hanoi (but not necessarily at Vietcong headquarters in the South) the non-Maoist view of General Vo Nguyen Giap apparently prevailed, whereas in China Lin Piao's September 1965 article on the people's war and the disappearance of General Lo in November signified the opposite outcome in China.

The Present Situation

By October 1, 1968, the revolutionary seesaw seemed to have bumped down firmly on the side of "law and order" as against revolutionary mass movements. The events of March-April may have represented a stand by the remaining leftists in the Cultural Revolution Group against the overweening success of the Army and civilian "moderates." At the least, it was an attempt to give a more revolutionary tinge to the Revolutionary Committees and the whole process of restoring order, in order to recuperate a proportion of the disillusioned leftist rebels at the lower levels. The official attacks on "polycentrism" invested with Mao's supreme authority a nationwide operation in which workers' teams were to put an end to the Red Guard type of faction fighting in educational institutions, factories, government offices, etc. The *Red Flag* article of August 25 ideologically justifying this was significantly signed by Yao Wen-yuan, who had sounded the first note of the cultural revolutionary opera with his article against historian Wu Han, a henchman of Mayor Peng.

The "moderate forces" associated with Chou En-lai now appear to hold a strong position. His triple power base comprises the government machine, the secret police under Hsieh Fu-chih, and an "old boy net" of military leaders still in uniform who formerly belonged to the New Fourth Army (1941 to 1945) and the Third Field Army (1946 to 1949) or to the "Fourth Front Red Army," which clashed with the First Front Red Army of Mao and Lin Piao when it passed through Szechuan during the Long March in 1935. Disgraced on arrival at the Yenan base, most of its cadres joined the One Hundred Twenty-Ninth Division of the Eighth Route Army (Commander Liu Po-cheng, Second in Command Hsu Hsiang-chien, Political Commissar Teng Hsiao-ping). Members of this group have been much denounced by the Red Guards and others. For example, the main culprit of the Wuhan mutiny and the commanders of Nanking and Foochow military areas—all old subordinates of Hsu in the "Fourth Front"—were blamed for obeying him instead of Mao. Hsu only reached the Politburo in August 1966 and Chou En-lai apparently "covered" him and his men.

All of Chou's six Vice Premiers and many of his other men in mufti are either old friends who studied together in France in the thirties or his colleagues in the New Fourth Army of Marshal Chen Yi (now Foreign Minister), who fits both categories. Although most of Chen Yi's old officers are in civilian government posts, they include the Vice Minister of National Defense and some important naval and military area officers. But Hsu's group includes five of the thirteen commanders of great military areas, including Peking, Nanking, and Foochow (opposite Formosa).

Another old "New Fourth" man is Politburo member

Marshal Nieh, a physicist and father of China's H-bomb. He is head of the State Council's Scientific and Technological Commission and deputy head of the Military Affairs Committee. It is possible that the purge of acting Chief of Staff Yang and other officers earlier in 1968 could well have been a move against Nieh and former members of his "North China Field Army" of 1946-54. In September, a group of senior nuclear and ballistic scientists were arrested as "Soviet agents." Shortly afterward there was an unsuccessful nuclear explosion, with rumors of sabotage. There have long been signs of a struggle for control of the "means of production" of modern weapons, which were originally isolated from political campaigns, including the Cultural Revolution. Now, after destroying the military cliques of Marshals Peng Te-huai and Ho Lung, the Cultural Revolution Group "left" or Marshal Lin may be attacking Marshal Nieh's "private kingdom," the next on the list. All of this suggests that the personal and factional power struggle at the center is not necessarily over. The triumvirate of Premier Chou, Marshal Lin, and the ultra-Maoist factions grouped around Mao's wife remains unstable.

In the country, the rebel organizations, disillusioned by the trend toward military rule, have not disarmed. Some have established sophisticated underground liaison systems. Some have adopted openly anti-Maoist positions, calling for a "new socialism" or a "second cultural revolution to overthrow the Communist Party." Others still wave the red flag to oppose the red flag. Liu Shao-chi has been officially (though unconstitutionally) declared to be overthrown, but the Party is still a force to be reckoned with. Having tried out the poorer peasants, the soldiery, and the teen-agers as agents of regeneration, Mao seems to be knocking the heads of the "intellectuals" and workers together, while there is talk now of reconstituting the Party and holding its Ninth Congress (due in 1963). The two and a half million soldiers, however well indoctrinated, are after all too thin on the ground to run the country. In practice they have often supported the wrong group when attempting to implement such vague orders as "support the left, but not any particular faction." It remains to be seen whether the present teams of workers, under Army leadership, will do any better than the Party "work teams" which were overwhelmed by events back in 1966.

At the end of October, the Central Committee (or part of it) met and issued a communiqué far less "revolutionary" in tone than its previous one of August 1966. In November, an old report of Mao's on the eve of victory in 1949 was republished with great fanfare; though accompanying editorials tried to make out that it was an inspired prophecy of the struggle against Liu Shao-chi, the actual text shows Mao calling for the same gradualist approach—in the collectivization of agriculture, for example—for which Liu is now denounced. Half of China's population is now under eighteen; though the turbulent students and other Red Guard gang fighters are being dispersed to remote areas, they cannot all be kept quiet on the farm once they have glimpsed the Paris Commune. Some of their clandestine publications suggest a Dubček-type humanization of Communism, others a degeneration into Nazism.

Mao himself has said that "China is not only the political center of world revolution, but should become the military and technical center, supplying weapons to the world's revolutionaries. By now China should be able to supply openly weapons marked in Chinese characters . . . and become the arsenal of world revolution." But there is an element of psychological compensation in this.

Ironically, the blustering success of Mao's "self-strength-

ening" of China has served to recreate rather than eliminate the old situation in which China invited foreign attack; even before Czechoslovakia, Mao feared the Soviets'
intentions but his defensive moves, based on false analo-
gies with a misinterpretation of his anti-Japanese war,
have served to attract, not repel, the danger. Moreover,
he believed that the "national malady of the pot of sand"
was cured by the anti-toxin of the Japanese war; must it
take another war before China's malady can be cured
definitively and she can join the world, having proved
that she can't beat it? Since the nature of any new generation of leaders is so problematic, we "foreign devils"
would do well to implement the policy of "containment
but *not* isolation" which the "devil we know" is still around
to deal with in Peking.

The Prospects of the Cultural Revolution

John Gittings

By the end of 1968, after two and a half years of Cultural Revolution, a comparative state of calm had been restored throughout most of China. This does not mean that the Cultural Revolution has succeeded, nor that the Maoists have won; even the Chinese were unable to provide a precise definition of what would constitute success or victory. Was it the overthrow of China's Head of State, Liu Shao-chi, and of those who were described as his agents? Was it the radical and total transformation of Chinese society along the lines of the Paris Commune which seemed to be Mao's ultimate vision? Or was it the much more limited objective of carrying out a rectification of the Chinese Communist Party? All three definitions were advanced at different times, yet only the first can be said to have succeeded. The second proved a dismal failure, while the third was barely under way as 1968 drew to a close.

Whatever the purpose was supposed to be, the reality was quite different. In the fall of 1966, Mao had uncorked the spirit of revolution; the genie which emerged took the shape of the student Red Guards and of their grown-up counterparts, the "revolutionary rebels." At first they were given their heads, on the theory that those who made revolution were bound to make it in the right direction. But by early 1967, they had already begun to get out of hand; the question from then on was how to get the genie back into the bottle. How to control the means of revolution had already become more important than the end which the Cultural Revolution was supposed to achieve.

The problem was, to use the Maoist term, one of "contradictions." By stirring up the spirit of revolution, Mao had uncovered and given free expression to a whole host of hitherto suppressed contradictions in Chinese society; the rebel factions which were formed by the Red Guards represented distinct economic or political interest groups, even if they all looked the same at first. The real rebels were the "have nots" of China—the unemployed students, contract laborers, unskilled workers, and others who had had the worst deal so far, and who looked on rebellion as the way to remedy their lot. The more conservative rebels were those who stood to gain by defending the status quo, those with good jobs and secure prospects who felt threatened by the upsurge of "revolution from below." All, of course, called themselves Maoists.

Left and Right

The same divisions, between radicals and conservatives, extremists and moderates, Leftists and Rightists (to use the terms which have now become familiar in Western writing on the subject, although they are all inexact), appeared at every level of society, including the top leadership in Peking, where many who had hitherto gone along with the Cultural Revolution now began to back away. The Left, represented by Mao himself, his chosen successor and Minister of Defense Lin Piao, and his wife, Chiang Ching, with her somewhat motley group of Cultural Revolutionaries, believed in sharpening the contradictions even further. Let the masses rebel as they please (with some guidance from us); the result must, dialectically speaking, be a "good thing": without destruction there can be no construction! So spoke the genuine Maoists. The Right, larger but less well organized than the Left, consisted in effect of those who wanted less rather than more revolution, and who asked despairingly where it would all end. Allegiances shifted frequently between the two ends of this political spectrum, but in general the Right could be said to include most of the Army leaders, the professionals in the Party and government, and perhaps—although he never came down squarely on their side—Premier Chou En-lai.

By the end of 1967, after a series of wild lunges to the Left, the moderate voice seemed to prevail; perhaps even Mao himself had temporarily lost some of his ardor. But if so, it was a case of *reculer pour mieux sauter,* and the spring of 1968 saw another "great leap" toward unfettered revolution. Once again by the autumn of 1968, cooler heads seemed to be in charge, this time with much greater authority than before, and the genie of revolution was being firmly rammed back into the bottle.

This Leftist resurgence in 1968, and the way in which it was eventually contained, is of crucial importance in attempting to understand how the Cultural Revolution has operated, and what are the rules of the game for the participants. If the whole affair were simply a "power struggle," as is sometimes said to be the case, the Left would have been slapped down long before, since the Right with its strength in the Army and Party commands most of the battalions. But the Left, weaker in numbers and strength, was armed with the authority of Mao and his formidable wife, and somehow managed to tip the balance once more in their own direction in this revolutionary seesaw with the more moderate forces. And it is because of this phenomenon that even at the end of 1968 many outside observers hesitated to predict a final end to the Cultural Revolution, even though the chances of yet another Leftist swing seemed very remote.

Back in the winter of 1967, most China Watchers had been more confident in their predictions. There had been quite a substantial "return to normality," to use one of their inescapable catchphrases. All the right things were being said: the Party should be reorganized, the great majority of its cadres should be rehabilitated, mass organizations should sink their differences by forming "great alliances." The Army should not be criticized, and the warring Red Guards should surrender their illegally acquired weapons. Students should return to school and stop wandering around the country; workers should go back to work and observe proper discipline. People should criticize themselves before attacking others. "Factionalism" and "anarchism" were unequivocally bad. It was all very high-minded and praiseworthy, with an emphasis on personal regeneration and collective therapy which reminds one of the Moral Rearmament Association—the Mao-study class having its counterpart in the group meeting, although in less luxurious surroundings.

But did it bear much relevance to the actual situation on the ground, or was it able to do more than contain temporarily the divisive forces unleashed a year before by the Cultural Revolution? The fragile nature of this revolutionary "pause" (which, like the bombing "pause" of North Vietnam, was always much less complete than appeared at first sight) was exposed by the events of spring and summer of 1968. In January and February the Left-

ist forces in Peking seemed to have their backs against
the wall. Yet the months of March to May saw a new
swing to the Left, and a quick response to it from the
revolutionaries in the provinces, leading to a resurgence
of violence—localized but severe—which threatened to
match that of the previous summer. The Leftist signals
emanating from Peking were confused and difficult to
read; they were ignored or distorted by many provincial
leaderships; they must have been anathema to the great
majority of Army leaders—nominally in control of large
chunks of the country's political and administrative apparatus. But it was still enough to upset the applecart.

Factionalism

In theory there was no reason why this new "opening
to the Left" should ever have occurred. Both in Peking
and in the provinces, the forces of moderation commanded
sufficient strength, in terms of administrative and military
power, to prevent its happening. But the turbulent events
of the previous summer appear to have eroded their self-
confidence, while the revolutionary élan of the Leftists
was diminished but never irrevocably quenched. Thus
although "factionalism" was officially condemned, the
directives from Peking, which called for the abolition of
nationwide Red Guard organizations, an end to their
itinerant travels, a return to school, and (in the case of
graduates) migration to the countryside, were only partially observed. The highly sophisticated networks of liaison and communication which had been set up in the
previous year between the various factions were now
frowned upon, but simply went underground. Students

continued to rove around the countryside claiming that "we would rather be wandering about, free and unrestrained."

For lack of a clear directive to suppress the factions, the Army, and what survived of the old Party establishment, found itself involved in a frustrating power conflict with the "rebels," centering on the creation of the new provincial Revolutionary Committees. On paper the moderates scored a resounding victory: all of the twelve Revolutionary Committees set up between January and April in 1968 were dominated by them, and they successfully resisted claims by the "rebels" that they were entitled to equal representation. But that was not the end of the story. The excluded rebels in many cases refused to accept the new Committees as the final solution, which they were intended to be, claiming that they "did not represent our views and are therefore null and void," lobbying to increase their own representation, or boycotting them altogether on the grounds that they merely amounted to "another kind of bourgeois rule."

Another problem was the reluctance of local officials, many of whom had been badly shaken by their treatment at the hands of the rebels not so long before, to act decisively. Schoolteachers complained that "we are afraid that we might say the wrong thing," cadres in the countryside were accused of "thinking of their mistakes behind closed doors," and Army leaders felt impelled at least to keep up the appearance of "supporting the Left."

In Peking itself, the "coalition" between Army and moderate civilian leaders, which some China Watchers believed was running the show, seemed to run out of steam. Perhaps the truth was that no formal coalition ever existed, and the winds of moderation could only blow as long as they were sanctioned by Mao. In spite of all that had happened, Mao's authority, as communicated through his chosen "close comrades," was still sufficient to command the respect of the moderates against their better judgment. Another theory is that the moderates had in fact been too successful. By the middle of February, only five of the original seventeen members of the Cultural Revolution Group still survived (Chen Po-ta, Chiang Ching, Chang Chun-chiao, Yao Wen-yuan, and Kang Sheng). The radical members who had come to the fore in the previous summer had been denounced as "ultra-Leftists," including Wang Li (charged among other crimes with responsibility for the sacking of the British mission in August), Chi Pen-yu (one of the chief editors of *Red Flag*), Mu Hsin, and Kuan Feng. According to this theory, the surviving Leftists now felt that their own future was at stake.

The Peoples Liberation Army (PLA), basking in the limelight of a series of receptions by Chairman Mao, and dominating the new Revolutionary Committees, may also have tipped the balance of power too far in its own direction for safety. In the state administration, some officials unwisely sought to launch a counterattack on the Leftists, notably in the Foreign Ministry, where a group of ninety-one ambassadors and senior cadres banded together to issue a statement in defense of Chen Yi—only to be disavowed by the wily Chen, who realized that they had gone too far.

The moderate trend was reversed dramatically at the end of March with the dismissal of PLA Acting Chief of Staff Yang Cheng-wu, Air Force Political Commissar Yu Li-chin, and Peking Garrison Commander Fu Chung-pi, and a rash of poster attacks upon prominent Vice-Premiers, including Nieh Jung-chen, Tan Chen-lin, and Li Fu-chun. The whole affair was dominated by Mme. Mao Tse-tung (Chiang Ching) amid fervent protestations of loyalty to her which suggested that there was more to it than met the eye. The official grounds for the dismissal of this military trio—that they had plotted against the "Party Center"—were based on very sketchy evidence, although there is some indication that Yang had exalted ideas of his own position, and had trodden on too many toes—both on the Left and the Right—including those of his own superior, Minister of Defense Lin Piao. But whatever the actual facts of the case, the propaganda which surrounded it suggested, if not a swing to the Left, at least a readjustment toward a more "revolutionary" line. It was now implied that the Army should not attempt to run the Cultural Revolution show by itself, that the "rebels" should be given a larger say in the Revolutionary Committees, that the "class struggle" should be intensified, and that the Committees themselves should take care not to become "divorced from the masses." This new line was, in effect, an attempt to inject a more revolutionary flavor into the whole process of political consolidation and restoration of order, without tipping the scales toward the kind of extremism which had been experienced in the previous summer.

By the end of April, the Leftist stimuli from Peking had become much more pronounced, and were reflected in the composition of the three Revolutionary Committees which were set up in May (Shensi, Liaoning, and Szechwan), all containing a much higher proportion of "rebels" in their leadership core. At the May Day celebrations in Peking, Chiang Ching shot up in the name list from nineteenth to ninth place, immediately followed by her fellow Cultural Revolution Group colleagues, Chang Chun-chiao and Yao Wen-yuan.

In the previous week, an article by the *Red Flag* commentator had offered a subtle, and dangerous, redefinition of "factionalism," which was no longer a bad thing in itself. "Proletarian factionalism" was now to be encouraged, and the "petty bourgeoisie" (often a synonym for the student Red Guards) was described as a potential ally of the revolutionaries. This must have come as manna from heaven to the dissident factions in the provinces, who could now practice "genuine proletarian factionalism" with a clear conscience.

But the swing to the Left was by no means unequivocal, and the confused editorials emanating from Peking, together with the equally confused response from the provinces, indicated a chaotic picture of internal dissent and sheer muddle. Only a few provinces welcomed the new definition of factionalism, urging in one case (Kweichow) that "revolutionary rebels" should have "absolute predominance in the Revolutionary Committees." Other provinces kept silent, or championed the claims of the "revolutionary cadres," or stubbornly continued to denounce the "extreme Left," paying only the barest lip service to the claims of the "rebels." The moderate Vice-Premiers hung on, with some difficulty, to their places on the official list. The joint editorial issued in Peking on May 16, the second anniversary of the start of the Cultural Revolution, was ambiguous on the question of factionalism, placing the Army, cadres, and rebels on equal footing in the Revolutionary Committees, and including a warning against "anarchism and sectarianism."

In retrospect this flurry of Leftist hyperbole in the months of April and May must be seen more as a rear guard guerrilla action by the radicals than as a demonstration of strength. But as long as the leadership in Peking was disunited, and the provincial leaders waited to see which way the ball would bounce, the factional rebels made hay while their Red Sun in Peking still seemed to shine.

Opinion is divided among outside observers as to the real extent of the violence which erupted in the summer

months of 1968. It was certainly intense in two provinces
on which there is detailed information—Kwangsi and
Kwangtung. Tibet also appears to have been thrown once
again into turmoil. Reports from Shensi and Chekiang also
suggested a serious deterioration of law and order. The
overall picture of violence may well have been much less
dramatic and widespread than that which had occurred
a year before, but this was not a very comforting thought,
for the country's ability to absorb even a lower level of
violence—the second time around—was also correspond-
ingly less. The Leftist resurgence never looked as if it was
causing total chaos, as it did for a time in 1967, and judged
by this standard it might be regarded as having exploded
with a whimper rather than a bang, but to those in the
near vicinity it still made quite a big noise.

The disorders, and the political confusion at the center, brought about a two-month-long hiatus (June and
July) in the establishment of Revolutionary Committees
in the remaining "hard core" sensitive areas of Fukien,
Yunnan, Kwangsi, Tibet, and Sinkiang. The chief military
and political leaders of these areas were sitting in Peking,
negotiating with each other and by telephone with their
localities in order to break the deadlock.

The month of July saw a more determined crackdown
upon the rival factions. A series of stern directives was issued from Peking, calling for an end to violence, restoration of communications, and the surrender by the factions to the PLA of their illegal weapons. Each directive
was addressed to a particular province, but local leaders
elsewhere were quick to interpret them in a nationwide
context. Red Guard organizations began to be dissolved
"voluntarily," students to be packed off "up to the moun-
tains and down to the countryside" (in some cases to
work on PLA farms), and the term "class enemies" began
to be used as a euphemism for the ultra-Left factions,

who were summarily dealt with if they refused to submit to discipline.

Decline of the Left

The new drive against the Left was less dramatic than that of September 1967: there was no nationwide directive of the kind which had been issued (and endorsed by Chiang Ching herself) on the fifth of that month, but it seemed likely to be more decisive. In the first place, the extreme Leftist "rebels" had probably lost much more public sympathy by this time, and their veneer of revolutionary idealism was beginning to wear rather thin. They also had fewer friends at court, and had made many more enemies in their own provinces. Second, the piecemeal approach which was adopted, starting with the provinces worst hit by violence, rather than seeking to pacify the nation overnight, was calculated to divide and weaken the Leftist opposition. And whether this indicated caution or compromise, there were no attacks upon the Leftists in Peking itself. It almost looked as if the Cultural Revolution Group had been guaranteed personal immunity from the anti-Leftist trend.

Perhaps the most significant difference between the two years was that on the latter occasion it was possible to invoke Mao's own authority for the new course of action. In his interview on the night of July 27-28 with student leaders in Peking, Mao appeared to turn his back upon those who had been his chosen vessels of Cultural Revolution, lambasting the students for having let him down. Army Day on August 1 was greeted with declarations of "absolute obedience" to the PLA, and on August 5 the *People's Daily,* denouncing the danger of "polycentrism" in the country, called for one hundred per cent obedience to the voice of Peking.

But Mao's approval for the suppression of the Left which now ensued may also have been dictated by overwhelming necessity. The crackdown had been operating with some severity in southern China, especially in Kwangtung, since June, and some observers believed that in many parts of the country the Army's patience had already worn dangerously thin. Apart from their irritation at the continuing factional violence, Army leaders may also have been concerned that their defensive capability on China's frontiers was badly weakened by the Cultural Revolution. Some border forces had been depleted in order to provide troops for the task of "supporting the Left," and it was only the crackdown in August which enabled them to return to their duties.

The official attacks on "polycentrism"—on those who defy central directives, claiming that they are the "center" of authority in their own locality—could be interpreted as another veiled attack upon the defiant Leftist rebels. But the theme was plugged so insistently as to hint at the existence of a polycentrist target higher up in the leadership echelon, perhaps among provincial Army leaders or even in Peking. An editorial in the Shanghai *Wen Hui Pao* of August 6 referred ambiguously, in this connection, to those polycentrists who argued that "so-and-so is not equal to the Central Cultural Revolution Group."

The crackdown in August got off to a flying start. Teams of workers and peasants, with Army backing, moved into China's schools and colleges and all other places (including factories and government offices) where factional disorder was still rife. The operation assumed massive proportions. Kwangtung province set a target of a "million-strong propaganda team" to fan out to all the trouble spots; in Kweichow, up to ten per cent of workers from any one factory were authorized to take part.

This new move was blessed by the Chairman, who bestowed a symbolic gift of mangoes upon the first workers' team operating in Peking's Tsinghua University. A growing mood of anti-intellectualism, supposedly aimed at bourgeois intellectuals but clearly directed at the new type of revolutionary intellectual thrown up by the Cultural Revolution, was accompanied by a rapid downgrading of the role of the Red Guards. It was now the working class which should play the "leading role" in the Cultural Revolution, and the worker-peasant teams were authorized to occupy the schools and other Red Guard centers on a permanent basis. The climax was reached in an article published on August 25 by Yao Wen-yuan, whose pen had struck the first blow in the preliminary stage of the Cultural Revolution by his attack on the historian Wu Han, but who now criticized the shortcomings of the Red Guards and urged them to submit to discipline. Meanwhile, the final five Revolutionary Committees were set up, their differences magically resolved, and by September 5 the twenty-nine provinces and other major Chinese areas could at last lay claim to "all-Red" status.

Peking Alarm

But by early September the pace and ferocity of the crackdown had begun to alarm the leadership in Peking —or at least those members of it most closely associated with Mao. The new line which emerged in yet another "latest instruction" from Mao, and in the pages of *Red Flag*, emphasized a more constructive approach to educational reform. Many bourgeois intellectuals had already successfully "remolded" themselves, the argument ran, and a "way out" should be provided for those who had not. Meanwhile there were clear signs of major divisions within the leadership. Both on Army Day and at the rally in Peking on September 7 to celebrate China's achievement of "all-Red" status, there were curious omissions in the leadership line-up and Mme. Mao's bad-tempered speech at the Peking rally indicated that she—and presumably her husband—were far from satisfied with the suppression of the Red Guards.

As winter drew near, a still uneasy but more workable relationship between the moderates and the Left—or, looked at from another perspective, between the provinces and the center—seemed to have been worked out. The essence of this compromise amounted to saving the Left's face by giving a radical tinge to policies which were essentially cautious. Thus the workers' and peasants' take-over of the country's schools was presented as a means for promoting educational revolution rather than a straightforward political device to tame the rebels. A centrally inspired movement to streamline the Revolutionary Committees and to send their members down to farms to "integrate themselves with the masses" also sounded radical enough, but it appeared to be used by provincial leaders to dispose of the more Leftist cadres. The campaign to rebuild the Communist Party, which began to pick up steam in October, also had a radical gloss to it. "The waste should be expelled," said Mao, and "new blood should be taken in." But in practice the task of party "rectification" was placed firmly in the hands of the conservative-minded Revolutionary Committees, which possessed the power to expel, confirm, or recruit Party members and to veto all Party organizations. The principle of election from below was rejected, and workers rather than Red Guards were the source for new recruits.

National Day, on October 1, saw an even more blatant example of face-saving when Mme. Mao and her hench-men appeared in a solid phalanx at the head of the official roster of names, while three moderate Vice-Prem-iers were pushed further down the list. Yet nothing was said at the celebrations to indicate that the Left still ruled the roost. The Party Central Committee Plenum which was held at the end of October gave Mao the paper vic-tory which he had long been seeking—a formal decision to expel Head of State Liu Shao-chi from the Party and all his positions—but otherwise the plenum's communi-qué struck an eminently sober note. It was all very dif-ferent from the last plenum, held in August 1966, soon after the start of the Cultural Revolution, which had called for grass-roots democracy and unfettered faith in "the masses."

Yet there were still sufficient signs of discord, from re-calcitrant Leftists who refused to admit defeat, to inhibit any pat conclusion that the Cultural Revolution was now neatly sewn up and disposed of. For the events of 1968 only served to underline the fact that Mao and his small band of radicals could still exercise an influence out of proportion to their apparent political strength. Even if many provincial leaders now merely paid lip service to Mao's "supreme directives," the very act of doing so helped to nudge their policies in a more radical direction, and to revive the spirits of the Left. A comeback by the exiled students and their disbanded organizations hardly seemed likely, but the fact remained that the original grievances of China's "have-not" rebels had not been satis-fied by the Cultural Revolution and would continue to fester beneath the surface. Nor could it be automatically assumed that the Right—an awkward coalition of Army leaders, Party bureaucrats, and government administrators—would remain united, and amicably divide the spoils of office at the Ninth Party Congress, scheduled for 1969.

Those who believe that the Cultural Revolution is in essence a massive "power struggle" have been partly justified by the evident factionalism which has divided China from the uppermost level of leadership downward. But the picture is further complicated by the continuing role of ideology and Mao's still potent though perhaps diminishing charisma. And the hornet's nest of grass-roots dissent which the Cultural Revolution has stirred up will also complicate any genuine "return to normality." Indeed, too many old wounds have been reopened, or new ones created, for the *status quo ante* ever to be restored. Hesitantly we may predict that life should be quieter for the Chinese in the near future, but we may more confidently assert that, in the long run, life will never be quite the same again.

"Revolution Within a Revolution?"

Ray Wylie

I had been in China for over a year when I decided to break my two-year contract and return to Canada. I explained to the new "revolutionary" authorities at the institute where I taught that although my stay in China had been very rewarding, it would perhaps be best if I left early. After all, there had been no teaching for several months, yet I had continued to draw a full salary.

The authorities, a "rebel" cadre and a "rebel" student, assured me they would consider my request carefully, and promised to come to see me again the next day. They did, and informed me that I was quite free to leave China at any time, but that they would be sorry if I left prematurely. They pointed out that China was experiencing an unprecedented political movement, and that few foreigners were on hand to see it with their own eyes. They felt that the Cultural Revolution was being slandered abroad, and that people around the world were being given a false picture of what was really happening in China.

This being the case, they hoped I, who had shown some sympathy toward the Chinese Revolution, would agree to stay on until the end of my contract and learn as much as possible about the Cultural Revolution. In fact, they suggested that my real job in China was no longer to teach English, but to educate myself about the Revolution. "In this way," they concluded, "you can tell Canadians the truth about what is going on in China." After some consideration, I agreed to stay. As to whether I would be able to discover the "truth" about the Cultural Revolution, however, I was not so certain.

Indeed, the discovery of anything resembling "truth" concerning China is a rare event at best. There is a great shortage of "hard facts," the information available is often obscure or unreliable, and the subject itself more often provokes emotion than stimulates inquiry. As a teacher living in China, however, I was given more access to what was going on than is the case with most foreigners, especially diplomats, correspondents, and tourists. I traveled extensively and visited many different types of organizations, from universities to mental hospitals. There were limits, of course, but I believe I saw as much of China as any foreigner can see.

Although I had studied Chinese for a year before going to China, I seldom had the opportunity to use it in natural situations. With a few exceptions English was my working language in China. My students and fellow teachers could speak it fairly well, and it was from them that I learned a good deal about what was going on in the country.

Making Sense

What is one to think of the Cultural Revolution? Is it, as the Maoists claim, a great political struggle to preserve the revolutionary character of the Chinese Revolution? Or is it, as many Western commentators apparently be-

lieve, nothing but a cynical struggle by an aging dictator
to maintain power?

Everything considered, I believe the Cultural Revolution must be seen within the context of the Chinese Revolution itself. Viewed in this light, it makes sense, just as
the whole Chinese Revolution, in spite of its shortcomings,
makes sense. What we are seeing is, in essence, a revolution within a revolution, with Mao Tse-tung attempting
to preserve the revolutionary character of the Chinese
Revolution, to prevent it from coming to a halt before its
basic goals have been achieved. One's attitude toward
the Chinese Revolution in general will of course shape
one's attitude toward the Cultural Revolution in particular.

Like most social upheavals, the Cultural Revolution has
occasioned a good deal of violence, although the foreign
press appears to have exaggerated its extent. "Excesses"
were committed on all sides, and a fair amount of violence
was tolerated by all parties concerned. In China, as elsewhere, most people do not seem to reject the use of violence in itself. Rather, they distinguish between "good"
and "bad" violence. In modern parlance, this would be
"revolutionary" and "counterrevolutionary" violence.

I well remember one incident which indicated to me
that violence, in the minds of many people, can be justi-
fiable, or at least acceptable. One morning, my wife and I
were riding downtown in a pedicab at the height of the
Cultural Revolution in Shanghai. We turned a sharp cor-
ner, and came across a middle-aged man being hounded
through the streets by a crowd. The man was probably an
official of some kind, although this is conjecture. Noticing
the concern and obvious distaste on our faces, the pedicab
driver, a grizzled man of over fifty, turned round to reassure us: "Don't worry about it. In the past he oppressed
(us)."

To our driver, the treatment meted out to this official was a kind of rough justice. It was a way ordinary people like himself could get back at the officials who had previously been untouchable. If certain excesses resulted from the application of "people's justice," he for one was not going to worry about it. As far as I could judge, millions of his fellow countrymen shared this general attitude.

Time for Assessment

Now that the Cultural Revolution appears to be settling down, people all over China are doubtless asking themselves if it was really worthwhile. After all, the costs have been rather high, including deaths, property damage, economic dislocation, loss of two years' formal education, and so on. A thoughtful Red Guard might ask himself, "What have we to show for it?"

The ultimate success or failure of the Cultural Revolution hinges on the answer Mao Tse-tung and his supporters give to this question. If Mao's response affirms the expressed promises of the Cultural Revolution, then he will have fully justified the people's faith in his vision and his leadership. But if his response denies these promises, we can only conclude that the people's faith has been misplaced, and that they will transfer their allegiance elsewhere, or submerge it in cynicism. It will be some time, however, before we can come to a valid conclusion.

What can we say now about the Cultural Revolution? As far as the actual struggle for power is concerned, it appears that Mao and his supporters have emerged victorious over their opponents both within and without the Communist Party. This victory is of course very important, for without it Mao would find it impossible to carry out the policies which he feels are essential if the country is to progress along socialist lines. The struggle for power is not only a struggle for position. More important, it is a struggle for policy, a struggle between two lines of action. As my students explained it, the "revolutionary" line of Mao Tse-tung has triumphed over the "revisionist" line of Liu Shao-chi. If this is true, I do not think we should expect any softening of the current Chinese attitude toward either domestic or foreign affairs, if by "softening" we mean some degree of movement toward Soviet-style revisionism.

Mao's Expectations

Over and above the maintenance of his own revolutionary line, and the political elimination of his opponents, Mao appears to expect more of the Cultural Revolution. Open criticism of the system by the people was encouraged—criticism within limits, I should add—and much of it was readily forthcoming. Students claimed they should have more say in their schools and universities, workers demanded that the system of payment by piecework should be abolished, and peasants proposed that more should be done to provide adequate social and cultural facilities in the countryside. My students told me that all of these criticisms are being noted by the new "revolutionary committees" which have temporarily replaced the former Party structures. When the Cultural Revolution settles down, they maintained, efforts will be made to remedy the shortcomings.

In fact, it appears that a good many reforms are going to be attempted in the near future, and some seem to have been carried out during the course of the movement itself.

On visits to many factories, for instance, I was consistently told that piecework had already been abolished at the workers' demand. Obviously, every demand cannot be met immediately. In Shanghai, for example, many workers asked for higher wages and better fringe benefits. Although some adjustments may well be made, it would be unrealistic to expect the government to satisfy these demands completely. Urban workers already earn more than the peasants, whose needs should receive priority. Moreover, the economy cannot withstand excessive pressures if steady growth is to be maintained. It is a truism that reforms will have to come within the limits of existing political, economic, and social conditions.

For the People

But Mao and his supporters seem to be interested in more than specific socio-economic reforms. Indeed, they appear determined to reform the political system itself. Mao is clearly a populist, and has a strong belief in the essential goodness of the common people, whom he knows well. He not only believes that the state should be run in their interest, but also that they themselves should have a say in how it is run. However, Mao is by no means an anarchist. He does believe that strong leadership is both necessary and desirable. If government is to be effective, there must be a balance between the need for leadership and the desirability of grass-roots participation in the political life of the nation.

Mao feared that this balance was being jeopardized by the rise of the Communist Party as a new bureaucratic elite. The Party was becoming "divorced from the masses," falling under the spell of revisionism, and preparing the way for the emergence of a new class system in China. Thus, the Maoist press declares that the Cultural Revolution is directed against those persons who are in effect "taking the capitalist road," those who consciously or unconsciously are moving away from the socialist egalitarianism of the early Revolution. As my students explained it, the precondition of a gradual return to a new class society is the emergence of the Communist Party as a self-conscious bureaucratic elite, working for its own interests instead of the interests of the people.

In launching the Cultural Revolution, it seems that Mao has attempted to prevent the emergence of a bureaucratic elite by reaffirming the egalitarianism of the early Revolution. That is, a healthy balance between the leaders and the led must be restored by strengthening the position of the people vis-à-vis the powerful Party and government structures. In the university where I taught in Shanghai, for example, the prestigious Party committee was dissolved and a new provisional organ of power—the "joint command"—was established in its place. Where the Party committee had been made up of Party members only, the "joint command" comprised representatives of the various social groups within the university, including Party members and cadres, students, faculty, administrative staff, and ordinary workers on the campus.

This new governing body was distinctly more "representative" of the people than the former Party committee had been. At the time I left China, in July 1967, the "rebel" students and "revolutionary" cadres appeared to be the most powerful forces on the new committee, but the other groups seemed to have some influence as well. The "joint command" also appeared to be more "responsible" than the Party committee, for its members were supposed to report back to their own organizations. In addition, the members were subject to recall by their own organizations if they proved unsuitable. It is too early to tell, but it is possible that these new governing bodies springing up all over China will be the basis of an improved political system.

Restructuring

It does not follow that the Communist Party will be scrapped. Indeed, Mao has already indicated that the Ninth Congress of the Party will be called in the near future. In essence, it appears that Mao wants to keep the Party as the guiding force in Chinese politics, but feels it must be restructured so as to permit a certain amount of popular control over it. Unfortunately, there is a distinct possibility that the restraints placed on the Party's power may be more ideological than institutional. Certainly, if the restraints are to be effective they must be given teeth, and this implies some basic structural changes. We can only wait and see what they will be.

But whether or not reforms are eventually realized, the fact remains that the Chinese people have probably been changed as a result of the Cultural Revolution. Mao firmly believes that the most important changes are in people's minds. If the political system is to be reformed people's minds must likewise be reformed. Unless the Cultural Revolution has taken place in the minds of the people, we cannot really say that it has taken place at all.

What of the People?

Thus the question poses itself: Were the people's minds "transformed" during the course of the Cultural Revolu-

tion? We must be realistic about this. We are not asking
if the Chinese people were *completely* transformed, or if a
totally new man has emerged during the course of the past
three years. These questions are idealistic, and not relevant to the understanding of the Cultural Revolution, or
any other revolutionary process. But it does seem that in
their understanding of politics and government, and in
their attitude toward authority, the Chinese people will
never be the same as a result of the Cultural Revolution.
As the Chinese phrase it themselves, their "political con-
sciousness" has been raised.

I can speak personally of my own students. Before
plunging into the Cultural Revolution, most of them were
both naive and ignorant about their political system. They
had been taught to respect and obey the Communist Party,
not to question its policies or treat its authority lightly.
Consequently, they had little understanding of the actual
political process: how policies were formulated, how ap-
pointments or important decisions were made. They believed China was being guided by "good" men who were
doing the best they could. Idealism the students had in
large measure; understanding was in shorter supply.

The Cultural Revolution has changed all this appre-
ciably. These same students have experienced a gigantic
struggle which will affect them for the rest of their lives.
Boys and girls organized themselves for political action,
openly challenged the Party's authority, pulled officials
from their high positions, and engaged in heated debate
on the question of China's future. Obviously, the experience of each individual was not the same, but the general
effect was apparent. In the course of this great upheaval,
my students received a political education which their
universities could never have offered.

Of course, it is true that the Cultural Revolution is being carried on within the limits of "Mao Tse-tung's

thought"—Sinicized Marxism-Leninism. Mao seems to enjoy a great deal of popular support, although it is equally apparent that he also has a number of enemies. In any case, Mao's thought is flowing into the vacuum created by the disintegration of traditional Chinese social philosophy. Mao's teachings are fast becoming the basis of a new Chinese social philosophy and ethical code, and the Confucian China of the past is gradually being transformed into the Maoist China of the future. As one elderly Party official explained, "Mao Tse-tung's thought is the only yardstick for the construction of a new socialist China."

During the Cultural Revolution the glorification of Mao Tse-tung and his thought reached new heights, much to the distaste of most foreign observers. But the cult of Mao is much more than the mere glorification of an individual. It is an effective means by which the Chinese people can accept a new "world outlook" that is substantially different from the one they previously held.

Future Revolution

The Maoist press has declared that there will probably be more Cultural Revolutions in the future. That is, the people have in Mao Tse-tung's thought the theoretical basis—and in the present Cultural Revolution the historical precedent—by which to justify an attack on any future régime that loses its revolutionary élan and begins to drift toward despotism. At the least, the specter of another Cultural Revolution will encourage China's future leaders to rule with an eye to the people's benefit. At the most, it will provide the people with a rationale for rebellion against a régime that becomes "divorced from the masses" and hence oppressive.

Much more than a mere struggle for power, the Cultural Revolution is, rather, a struggle for policy. It is an aging revolutionary's final attempt to prevent the Chinese Revolution from degenerating into a modern form of Oriental despotism. It is an effort to reaffirm the essential principles of egalitarian socialism in the face of the encroachments of class society. Above all, it is an endeavor to transform the very minds of the Chinese people, to impart to them the ideal of a "new China" and the idea that it is "right to rebel" if a future régime betrays that ideal. The present upheaval in China shares the strengths and weaknesses of all revolutionary movements—destruction and construction go hand in hand.

When the Communists achieved victory in 1949, Mao made it quite clear that the Chinese Revolution was by no means over. On the contrary, it had just begun. The acquisition of state power was only the first step in a "long march" of 10,000 miles. If, in the course of this uphill struggle, the ideals of the early Revolution are jeopardized, they must be reaffirmed. And if some of the old leaders waver in their determination to "carry the revolution through to the end," they must be removed from power. To Mao Tse-tung and his supporters, the dynamism of the Revolution must be maintained if a "new China" is to emerge. Hence the Cultural Revolution today, and the possibility of another tomorrow.

THE
ECONOMY

The economy of China, which may still be one of the countries with the poorest material standard of living in the world, has clearly suffered during the Cultural Revolution. So little hard information is available that the experts differ considerably in their assessments of the damage. Robert Dernberger considers in the following article the impact of the Cultural Revolution on the Chinese economy and discusses the economic policies that seem to be at issue between the two parties to the dispute. But the role of economic questions in the Cultural Revolution, and the claims of Mao as an economic theorist, are even more controversial among Western experts than the current state of China's economy. Jack Gray, in a second article, develops a less orthodox interpretation of recent events and argues that Maoism is above all a practical economic policy for an underdeveloped country in China's circumstances.

Economic Realities and China's Political Economics

Robert F. Dernberger

The Cultural Revolution was much more than a temporary interruption in Communist China's development program. In fact, any meaningful assessment of economic realities in China today must include a discussion of the different economic policies of the contending factions in the Cultural Revolution, the impact of the Cultural Revolution on the current state of the economy, and its effect on China's economic future. I propose to discuss each of these topics.

One little caveat must be made. Quite simply, with the advent of the Cultural Revolution and the complete blackout of meaningful quantitative economic data, the study of China's contemporary economy has become an art which relies heavily on intuition and common sense. Even if we disagree with Gunnar Myrdal's main theme in *Asian Drama*—that Western economic theory is inappropriate for a study of Asian economic development—the sophisticated techniques of modern Western economic analysis certainly are of limited use in a study of contemporary events in China.

Most of the informative journals in China have been either temporarily or permanently suspended. Wall posters and radio broadcasts provide meaty fare for sophists and speculators, but give little hope for a solid analysis of the current state of the economy. A somewhat detailed assessment could be based on the limited quantitative information available from the official sources, the downward biased estimates of agricultural output published by the U.S. Consulate in Hong Kong, and the intuitive or subjective reports of either the optimistic or pessimistic visitors to the mainland. Another source might be the sudden downturns or revivals in foreign trade reported by China's trading partners to indicate general economic conditions on the mainland. To make an assessment with confidence, however, the economist must argue that the tools of his profession give him a special vantage point, and the effective use of these tools requires the input of reliable, quantitative information.

Carl Riskin, in his review of the Chinese economy in 1967 (*Michigan Papers in Chinese Studies* [No. 2, 1968]) claims that the turmoil in China and the lack of quantitative data have forced economists to grope about like the blind men of the familiar tale in their attempt to describe the elephant. According to Riskin, some have become tired of groping and have begun presenting "ideal conceptions of elephant nature" as substitutions for the unavailable facts.

Since the description and analysis presented in this article agrees substantially with those of several other economists, especially that of Riskin and Dwight Perkins in his article on the economy published in the *China Quarterly* (April-June 1967), one could conclude that several blind men are describing the elephant after they have all grabbed hold of its trunk. But I do not believe an economist is "blind" because he lacks data. Rather, armed with the basic principles of his discipline, he is more like a one-

eyed giant in the land of the blind. The real question is,
How well does he see with that one eye?

Surplus Mouths to Feed

By any standards of common sense or economic analysis,
China is an underdeveloped country faced with the major economic realities of too many people who live on limited fertile land and whose average productivity is too
low. In the *Bulletin*'s special issue on China in 1966 I discussed how the specific problems of population growth,
the shortage of fertile land, the low level of voluntary savings, the limited domestic capabilities for capital accumulation, and the shortage of skilled and technical manpower served as constraints on China's ability to achieve
sustained economic growth. Because I believe most of that
discussion, under the title "Economic Realities," remains
valid today, I need only present some further elaborations
or corrections made necessary by the events of the past
two years.

Surplus labor is an asset in a rapidly developing country
which is also attempting to maintain a large labor-intensive military force. The real problem associated with
China's population is its rate of growth and the obstacles
involved in any attempt to organize and mobilize such a
large and widespread population under centralized control. During the agricultural crisis in 1959-61, of course,
the number of mouths to be fed outweighed the benefits
from having so many hands for production. The effect of
the agricultural crisis on the size of China's population
was a reduction of about fifty million in the "expected"
population increase—or a total population in 1965 of

about 725 million instead of 775 million. These fifty million Chinese did not starve to death, they simply were not born, due to the decline in per capita consumption of child-bearing age groups.

The Communists desire to reduce the birth rate by more humane means, however, and a vigorous birth control program has been waged in the urban areas since 1963. According to the estimate of Edwin F. Jones, research economist in the Department of State, this program has achieved significant results. Although the working-age population will increase by over two per cent a year during the next decade due to the relatively high birth rate in the 1950s, Jones estimates the birth rate will be less than two per cent and may even decline to less than 1.5 per cent by 1973. Nonetheless, even if the Chinese are able to reduce the birth rate to 1.5 per cent by 1973, about sixteen million people would still be added to the total population every year. Thus, the real solution remains the need to achieve sustained economic development, especially a rate of growth in agricultural production of about three per cent a year.

In 1966 I was naively optimistic in regard to the problem of organizing and mobilizing the Chinese population, claiming "the available evidence suggests that the agricultural crisis in 1959-61 seriously damaged the enthusiasm and morale of the Chinese people . . . but there is nothing to indicate that the Party has lost control." In fact, after two years of continual conflict, we now must ask who has control of the Party and to what extent the Party controls economic activity. The winner of this current conflict will once again face the difficult problem posed by the need to organize and mobilize over three-fourths of a billion Chinese.

Low Yields per Capita

A second major economic problem in China is the shortage of land that is presently available for use in agricultural production. The exceedingly high labor-to-land
ratio has led to the adoption of labor-intensive methods
of production resulting in high yields per unit of land,
but low yields per man. Of the several available means
to increase production—reclamation of land, mechanization, increased inputs of water and fertilizer, and reorganization of the peasants—the Chinese Communists concentrated on the latter option for increasing yields during
the 1950s, successively forming mutual aid teams, cooperatives, and Communes within a period of only eight
years. As I argued in my earlier article, "history shows
that these organizations do succeed in giving the government greater control over both the peasant and his output, but offers little evidence that they succeed in achiev
ing the required increases in output." The failure of the
Communes to solve China's agricultural problem seriously
increased the tension among China's leaders, who dis
agree over how that problem should be solved.

Following the agricultural crisis, top priority was given
to the need to increase agricultural output. Although the
Commune remains as an institution, the functional organization of agriculture has reverted to the pre-1958
pattern, i.e., the collective. In addition, greater efforts
have been made to increase inputs of fertilizer and to ex-
pand the irrigated area. Rural electrification is being expanded to facilitate the use of mechanical pumps. For
example, consumption of chemical fertilizer increased
threefold between 1960 and 1967, while eighty per cent

of the irrigated fields in the Yangtze delta were served by mechanical pumps in 1965.

The use of chemical fertilizer in China is still below the world average and is far below the average for Taiwan, Japan, or Korea. The examples provided by these countries, however, enable China to borrow available technology and to skip much of the costly experimentation and learning period already undergone by other countries in the Far East. The necessary inputs must be provided to the Chinese peasant and he must be induced to adopt this borrowed technology, but the potential for increased output is tremendous. For example, the achievement of Japanese rice yields of the pre-World War II period would increase China's output by ninety per cent, and China could more than double its output by achieving Japan's present rice yields. Taiwan's rice yields are even higher than Japan's. The increased use of fertilizer and water offers a proven means of obtaining sustained growth in agricultural production, and in the attempt to increase agricultural output as rapidly as possible, the presently available fertilizer and state investment are being concentrated in the stable and high-yield areas which market a large share of their total output. It is planned that stable and high yields will be achieved throughout the entire country in two or three decades.

Cost Factors

Land reclamation is very costly and the Chinese have not made any major efforts in this direction since 1957. Not only has the amount of land reclaimed or developed for agricultural production been relatively small in the past, but the total amount of farm land diverted for the use of various construction projects during the 1950s was about one-half the area added to cultivation through reclamation. Mechanization is still regarded by most Communists throughout the world as a long-run goal for agriculture, but it also is very costly and is not the most promising means of increasing yields *per unit of land* in a country with surplus labor.

The major economic problem in a developing country which a Communist government finds easiest to solve is the need to increase the rate of savings, yet there is no reason to believe the Chinese have significantly increased the "voluntary" rate of savings from a level of approximately five per cent. Through direct and indirect taxes and rationing, however, the government has been able to obtain "forced" savings and elevate the rate of savings for the economy as a whole to between twenty and thirty per cent. At this level, the government is able to divert a large amount of resources from the production of consumers' goods to the production of producers' goods, military equipment, and export. When agricultural output declined during the agricultural crisis in 1959-61, the level of savings also declined due to the need to maintain minimum standards of food consumption. On the other hand, the declines in agricultural production also led to a reduction in industrial production. Excess capacity in industry reduced the demand for producers' goods and, therefore, the level of investment also declined in 1961-63. As output revived in the mid-1960s, however, the need to increase savings and investment has again become an important economic reality in China.

Although the Chinese are still able to maintain a relatively high rate of savings and investment, the ease with which these savings can be obtained and the rate of growth resulting from the investment of those savings are somewhat less in the mid-1960s than in the 1950s.

In order to revive production in the 1960s, an incentive system was implemented which allowed producers to retain a greater share of their output, reducing the potential rate of savings available for state investment. Once a given amount of savings has been obtained by the state, the rate of growth realized from the investment of those savings will be less than was realized during the First Five-Year Plan period, since a much larger share of the total investment is now being devoted to the agricultural sector.

The fourth major economic reality in China is the low level of indigenous technical ability, namely, the difficulty in converting savings in the form of agricultural products and consumer's goods into investment or producer's goods. During the 1950s, the Soviet Union provided crucial material and technical assistance in helping China build and equip heavy industrial projects and by supplying China with metals, petroleum, etc. This assistance was financed partially by Soviet loans in the early 1950s, but was completely paid for by Chinese exports after 1954. The Soviet loans have now been repaid and China is currently maintaining a balance of exports and imports in foreign trade, a remarkable feat for a developing country.

Following the open break between China and the Soviet Union in 1960, China began to increase its imports of complete plants and technical assistance from the industrialized countries of West Europe and Japan, imports paid for and limited by China's export capacity. China has borrowed short-term capital from the non-Communist countries in the 1960s, mostly to finance imports of food grains. Thus, unless large-scale, long-term loans are obtained from abroad, China's economic development effort will depend on indigenous technical capabilities.

The unilateral withdrawal of Soviet technicians in 1960 was a severe blow to China's economic development effort, but this enforced self-sufficiency did result in a more rapid development of the necessary indigenous technical skills. The most dramatic evidence of this is in nuclear research. The first Chinese nuclear device was detonated in October 1964. Less than three years later tests had been made of a hydrogen bomb and nuclear-armed, short-range (400 miles) missiles. A test of a 2,000-mile-range missile is expected shortly and Cheng Chu-yuan estimates a 6,000-mile-range intercontinental ballistic missile will be available by 1970.

Less dramatic, but more important for China's economic development, are the increasing number of industrial plants being built and equipped without foreign assistance. While self-reliance is still a long way off, rapid strides in that direction have been made. It is in this area that the Cultural Revolution poses its greatest threat to China's economic development potential: the deterioration in the scarce stock of technical and managerial ability. Repeated attacks on "politically unreliable," "bourgeoisie corrupted," "revisionist," and "reactionary," yet skilled and capable individuals and the disruption of normal management and planning procedures are much more serious and more difficult to remedy than a temporary decline in the level of output.

Impact on the Economy

If one were to believe the frequent reports of armed clashes and sabotage in China's major industrial centers, one would conclude that China's economy is in utter chaos. Yet that economy continues to sustain one-fourth of mankind and supports the largest and most powerful military force in Asia. China still is an underdeveloped, agricultural country, and even in a chaotic situation, the economy will not "grind to a halt." On the other hand, the levels of output achieved by 1965, just before the Cultural Revolution, were not spectacular and did not leave the economy a margin sufficient to absorb any ill effects of the Revolution.

~In agriculture, grain output declined to a low point in 1960 (about ten to fifteen per cent below the level of output in 1957) and slowly increased to 200 million metric tons in 1964 (about ten per cent above the output). There was little or no increase in food grain output in 1965 and 1966. The main effort in the socialized sector in agriculture has always been concentrated on food grains, but economic crops frequently have failed to achieve significant increases in output and have almost always fallen far short of the planned level of output. Reports that economic crops in 1966 have surpassed the 1957 level of output are undoubtedly exaggerations. Edwin Jones estimates the output of cotton, the largest economic crop, in 1965 was still more than ten per cent below the 1957 level, and that the output of oil seeds also fell far short of the 1957 level. (The estimates of others are even lower.) The pig population, on the other hand, may well have recovered its 1957 level by the end of 1965.

The total value of agricultural production in 1966 probably was slightly higher than it had been nine years earlier. In the meantime, of course, there had been an increase of about 100 million in total population. Nonetheless, due to imports of food grains amounting to about five million tons a year beginning in 1961, the per capita availability of food grains in 1966 was not more than five per cent less than it had been in 1957. In 1965, led by the very significant increases in the output of chemical fertilizer, petroleum, steel, and electric power, the output of heavy industry was double that of 1957. The output of light industry, however, did not recover very rapidly due to the continued shortage of agricultural raw materials and was not much higher in 1965 than it had been in 1957. Thus, on balance, total industrial output probably was about fifty per cent larger in 1965 than it had been in 1957 and is reported to have increased by another twenty per cent in 1966.

In 1966, therefore, the Chinese economy had survived the serious economic crises of 1959-62 and had achieved a level of output in agriculture and industry which was possibly as much as one-third greater than nine years earlier in 1957.

This very brief summary of China's economic recovery provides a rough estimate of the level of economic activity in China on the eve of the Cultural Revolution. In general, it agrees with the much more detailed studies of agricultural and industrial output during this period by Robert M. Field, Kang Chao, Dwight Perkins, and Edwin Jones.

— Among China specialists, however, there is serious disagreement about whether food grain output actually did reach 200 million tons in 1964-66. According to the estimates of John Wenmohs, U.S. agricultural attaché in Hong Kong, food grain production merely regained the 1957 level of 185 million tons in 1964-65 and declined by almost five per cent in 1966. Thus, according to Wenmohs' estimates, and others, the per capita availability of food grains in 1966 was no higher than those levels experienced during the agricultural crisis in 1959-61.

In my opinion, even the high estimates do not present a very happy picture of living conditions in China. The high estimates for 1966 place the Chinese at a level of per capita availability of food grains that is only four per cent higher than has been estimated as a starvation level. In any event, contrary to the brief summary presented here, some specialists argue that China had not yet recovered from agricultural crisis when the Cultural Revolution began.

Conclusions drawn from the more pessimistic estimates of China's food grain production appear frequently in the press and are quoted to refute the account of developments in the 1960s presented here. But the per capita availability of food grains implied in the pessimistic estimates are not supported by the non-quantitative reports we have on conditions in China in 1965-66. There were no reports of another economic crisis and sufficient food supplies appear to have been available, at least in urban areas. Furthermore, we know the Chinese Communists increased the level of investment in agriculture in the 1960s, and it is hard to believe that, even though a much larger quantity of inputs, especially fertilizer, was being applied than in 1957, output was no larger or was even less.

Economic Uncertainties

What happened to the economy after 1966 is even less certain. Although the economy may have recovered from the agricultural crisis of 1959-61 and reached a peak in 1966, isn't it possible that the effects of the Cultural Revolution have led to a second economic crisis just as serious as the first one nine years ago? Daily reports on China from visitors, refugees, radio broadcasts, and China Watchers would certainly lead one to believe this has happened. I do not have sufficient evidence to refute this, and even if drastic declines in output have not yet taken place, they may well have occurred by the time this volume appears.

Nonetheless, based on evidence which I find plausible,

and discounting both the empty claims of "great leaps" in production made by the Chinese Communists and the "sky is falling" reports of some Western journalists and government officials, I believe the general conclusions of Cheng Chu-yuan as to the immediate impact and those of Dwight Perkins as to the long-run impact of the Cultural Revolution on the economy, both published in 1967, still to be valid. According to Cheng, "there were no signs of serious disruption in Chinese industrial and agricultural production at least until November 1966 . . . the disruptive effects of the political turmoil in some parts of the national economy seemed conspicuous in 1967; [and] if the current situation continues, the national economy could be damaged for years." According to Dwight Perkins, ". . . politics has impinged on economics during the past year and will continue to have some effect in the future, [but] barring the indefinite prolongation of political upheaval . . . the principal determinants of China's future economic growth will remain the rate of investment and the pace of development in agriculture." I would conclude that serious, yet temporary, disruptions have occurred in industry and transportation, but the farmers apparently are continuing, as they have for forty centuries, to prove their ability to survive both bad weather and bad government.

In the mid-1950s, the Chinese Communists often boasted of their having conquered nature. Yet the one variable which most affects the level of agricultural output is still weather conditions. The introduction of capital for water control or irrigation, fertilizer, and machinery introduces a growth trend in output, but weather conditions still account for most of the fluctuations in that trend. Since very favorable weather conditions prevailed throughout China and the Far East in 1967, there is reason to accept the Chinese claim of a bumper harvest, the high-

est in their history. Whether output of grains was as high
as 230 million tons is, of course, debatable. My own estimate would be approximately 215-220 million tons or an
increase of five to seven per cent. In 1968, weather conditions were not favorable.

Agricultural Decline?

Several arguments have been advanced to support the
claim that the Cultural Revolution has led to a decline in
agriculture. First, there is the argument that the Cultural
Revolution spilled over into the countryside in 1967 and
recollectivization began with the elimination or reduction
of the private plots in some Communes. This increased
recollectivization was assumed to have had a negative
impact on production. But the countryside does not yet
appear to have been disrupted by the Cultural Revolution,
and agricultural policy, administration, and institutions
seem basically the same as they were in the early 1960s.
This is not to deny that the peasants have been required
to spend a large amount of time studying the thoughts
of Mao. This may be the price they have paid for being
excluded from the turmoil of the urban areas. The Maoists,
of course, claim these study sessions increase productivity
—a unique case, if it works, of substituting ideology for
chemical fertilizer.

Transportation Disrupted

Second, there is the argument that although the Cultural
Revolution did not directly intervene in the agricultural

sector, it disrupted the transportation of inputs to, and weakened the cadres' control over, that sector. There is no question that the disruption of the transportation network seriously hampered a rational distribution of agricultural products, but I doubt that Chinese agriculture has advanced to the point where output depends upon inputs supplied by industrial centers or where disruption in the long-distance supply of chemical fertilizers would cause serious declines.

Based on China's experience in the past two decades, I would suggest decision making and direct control above the level of the production team is detrimental to output and, in general, the less interference with the production team the better. Judging from the institutional reforms introduced in Chinese agriculture after 1960, those responsible for reviving agricultural output following the crisis apparently agreed with this argument.

Third, the available indirect evidence of changes in imports of food grains is used as an indication of what has happened to current production. On the basis of contracts already signed or being negotiated, China plans on importing food grains over the next three years at least. This is not necessarily an indication of inadequate domestic production, as was true in the early 1960s. I believe it is based on the benefits or reduction in costs to be gained from storing domestic grain in the areas of surplus production and transferring it to other areas when the need arises, while importing foreign supplies of food grains for consumption in the coastal, urban areas. This is exactly the same pattern of grain distribution which China found most economical in the first half of the twentieth century. In any event, imports of food grains in 1967 were greatly reduced and thus these imports do not contradict a large increase in domestic production.

Declining Grain

The recently reported declines in Chinese shipments of foodstuffs to North Vietnam also are cited as evidence of a decline in Chinese grain output in 1968. But this is having our cake and eating it too. The United States has been bombing for almost three years in an attempt to destroy production in North Vietnam and the supply lines from China. Yet, upon a report of food shortages in North Vietnam, it is argued this reflects a decline in Chinese domestic production. Even *within* China, the distribution of grain has been disrupted due to the serious damage to the transportation network in the Cultural Revolution.

Fourth, the difficulty of extracting the desired level of grain surpluses from the rural area has been emphasized by reports of the Army assuming responsibility for this task and peasant raids on grain storehouses. The Army, however, has assumed a leading role in all areas of the economy, and one would expect an increase in the use of force to extract the grain surplus when the production team is given greater management and control powers and the power of the local cadre is weakened. One would also expect an increase in the need to protect and in attempts to break into these stocks when they are stored locally. Both phenomena are recurrent themes in Chinese history and do not necessarily indicate a decline in production.

We may conclude that 1967 was a very good agricultural year. In 1968, however, the agricultural supply situation was undoubtedly growing tense due to a decline in output and the continued disruption of transportation.

Economic Issues

China's major industries and industrial cities—Wuhan, Shanghai, and the industrial centers in Manchuria—have been the very centers of the Cultural Revolution, and industrial workers, along with the students, were the major non-Party elements involved. Thus, China's industry must have experienced at least a short-run or temporary decline. If past experience can be used as a guide, the poor agricultural years in 1965 and 1966 and the reported difficulty in extracting an agricultural surplus from that sector in 1967 would indicate a decline in the rate of increase of industrial production. The large increase in imports of producer's goods from West Europe in 1967, on the other hand, would indicate a large increase in industrial investment, if not output. The serious disruptions of transportation and the normal management and planning procedures in industry are certain to have seriously weakened effective planning in these sectors and must have reduced the ability of any enterprise to rely upon planned supplies of inputs.

These latter effects of the Cultural Revolution are much more serious and more difficult to cure than a temporary decline in output and are the greatest threat to China's long-range prospects for economic development. Technical and managerial abilities are China's scarcest resources, and the stock of these talents which have been built up over the past two decades is threatened with extinction. Physical capital can be rebuilt, the soil can be replenished, temporary declines in output can be made up through overtime, extra shifts, and the implementation of a material incentive system, but education, training, and ex-

perience call for a large investment of time as well as
resources.

The fate of the technicians and managers is itself a
major issue in the Cultural Revolution. There are, of
course, many different ingredients in the Cultural Revolution and I do not mean to imply that the violent struggle for power which has occurred in China during the
last two years is merely a debate over economic policy.
Radical ideology is an obvious element in the Cultural
Revolution, and we are forced to reexamine the accepted
interpretations of the whole history of the last twenty
years. Such a reexamination, I believe, reveals the continued existence of two opposing schools of thought, and
the history of Chinese Communist economic development policy is best understood as the alternating ascend-
ancy of these two schools.

I would expect the anti-Maoists would include those
who were given responsibility for administering the country and reviving the economy in the early sixties, while
the Maoists or radical ideologues were said to be concentrating on ideological matters and a cultural revolution
in the Army. There was, of course, no formal organization
or working coalition representing these opposing points
of view, but rather a consensus of interests in specific
policy discussions. It is quite possible, when faced with
changing economic and political situations, certain individuals agreed with one point of view on one occasion
and with the other on another occasion.

Two Schools

A more important and equally difficult task is to name
the two schools of thought and specify their essential ar-

guments. One school of thought is easy to name: the Maoists or radical ideologues who advocate the mass mobilization of manpower and constant struggle to transform man into a classless, unselfish, and dedicated member of society, able to rely on his own ability to solve the technological problems of development.

The opposite school of thought is easy to name only if we label it "anti-Maoist." The name is not entirely correct, however, as there were several periods in the last two decades when the two groups agreed on development strategy for China. Other terms, such as pragmatists, economists, rationalists, etc., have been used to describe the anti-Maoist approach to economic development, but these terms distort the principal disagreement between these two groups. While we may believe that one group is more pragmatic and rational than the other, it is best to analyze their differences without such value-laden or culturally oriented name-calling. Some of the arguments attributed to Mao's opponents and the names given to them as a group almost go so far as to indicate they are really advocates of the Chicago School of Economics.

A name frequently suggested for the anti-Maoist group is the planners. But planning refers to a particular tactic or institutional organization for development which could be supported by either group. For example, Sun Yeh-fang advocates the restoration of the law of value, i.e., proper price formation, in order to obtain a realistic or effective plan, while the Maoists hold that this is valid only in a capitalist economy and is an attack on socialist planning. Under socialism, the plan must regulate the economy, but must not be based on market values. Rather, it must be formulated under the direction of the thought of Mao. In the early 1950s, planning in Communist China referred to the implementation of the Soviet model. In essence, this model relies on the centralized allocation of resources determined on the basis of material balances in physical terms for the economy as a whole, the output of specific industries and sectors being determined and incorporated as the targets of annual and five-year plans. We are left, therefore, with the unhappy choice of the word "technologists" for the anti-Maoist approach to economic development.

Opposing Approaches

The technologist approach to economic development relies on the creation of a technical bureaucracy, somewhat unrestrained in the performance of their assigned tasks by the official ideology. Economic development policies, of course, would always be justified "by the general line of the party, the great leadership of Chairman Mao, and the principles of Marxism and Leninism," but the policies themselves would permit and even encourage the emergence of differences in material well-being and privilege. These differences would be closely associated with differences in technical ability.

Perhaps the best clarification of the distinction between the radical ideologists and the technologists can be made by examining just one of the many debates made public during the Cultural Revolution: the debate over the role of the trade unions. The radical ideologists criticized the trade unions for centering attention on production, for their emphasis on technical courses, for holding demonstrations of professional skills, for training workers in the basic skills, and for admitting workers with a bourgeois class background. Not only did all this training limit the worker's time for studying the thoughts of Mao, but the trade unions, according to the radical ideologues, were to serve as mass organizations of the proletariat class alone when they should be devoted to the class struggle, not the attainment of technical skills.

These opposing approaches to economic development, of course, did not originate with the Cultural Revolution, but existed at the very founding of the People's Republic in 1949. The first economic policy decision involved the launching of the land reform campaign—a radical ideological policy as initially implemented, but supported by both groups. In industry, the reliance on Soviet assistance and the adoption of the Soviet model was undoubtedly accepted by the radical ideologists as a necessary expedient for rapid industrial development. They did not accept, however, either the political or social implications of the Soviet model, and the first major debate between the two groups concerned the pace of socialization in the agricultural sector.

According to the technologists, the physical elimination of the landlords had greatly reduced the need for class struggle in the agricultural sector and "more orderly procedures" could be relied upon to organize the peasants and increase production. The long-run goal of the socialization of agriculture could proceed slowly and would be related to the mechanization program of agriculture.

The original target of the First Five-Year Plan, set in October of 1953, called for twenty per cent of all peasant households to be members of a producer's cooperative by 1957. Mao, on the other hand, realized it would take twenty to twenty-five years to complete the mechanization of agriculture and that "new rich peasants had already appeared everywhere" following land reform. At a conference of provincial Party leaders in July of 1955, Mao called for a rapid increase in the pace of collectivization and an intensification of the class struggle in the countryside. The technologists were accused of being like "women with bound feet," and early in 1956, Mao set the time limit for the socialization of agriculture as three or four years. This program of the radical ideologists was adopted by the Central Committee in October of 1955. Thus, only two months after the National People's Congress had formally adopted the Soviet model embodied in the First Five-Year Plan, the radical ideologists won a decisive victory in the Central Committee of the Party. By the end of May 1956, over ninety per cent of the peasant households were in cooperatives.

Soviet Aid to Industry

The initial success of the Soviet model in China was directly related to the continued rehabilitation and reconstruction of existing industrial facilities, large-scale Soviet financial, material, and technical assistance, very good agricultural years in 1952 and 1955, and the ability of the central government to gain an increased share of the slowly growing agricultural output by means of successive institutional changes in the agricultural sector. After 1955, however, further gains from these sources were not available.

China received no new Soviet loans after 1955 and was faced with the need to maintain an export surplus in the last half of the 1950s in order to repay the loans received in the first half. The existing industrial capacity had been rehabilitated and further increases in industrial output relied on increases in efficiency and bringing new plants into production. By the end of 1955, the central government had secured control over the available agricultural surplus through the implementation of compulsory grain deliveries and rationing, but the poor harvest in 1956 led to a decline in the agricultural surplus available to the central government in that year. Thus, although the advocates of the Soviet model optimistically drew up a Second Five-Year Plan in 1956, the First Five-Year Plan was already in trouble when it was formally adopted in 1955.

To alleviate these problems, the technologists began a series of reforms in 1956 which significantly modified the Soviet model in order to reduce the rigidity of centralized planning and allocation of resources and the strains placed on the economy by the overambitious First Five-Year Plan. A major wage reform was adopted, the ratio of investment in heavy industry to light industry was reduced, and greater freedom was given to enterprises for securing their inputs and distributing their output, a movement which paralleled to some extent the creation of free markets in the agricultural sector. In 1957, the investment program was reduced and the pace of industrial development was slowed down. The Great Leap Forward or Commune movement of 1958 represents a complete victory for the radical ideologists and a rejection of the Soviet model which was already being modified by the technologists in 1956 and 1957.

Almost by default, the technologists were provided an opportunity to implement their economic policies when they were given responsibility for reviving the economy following the failure of the Great Leap Forward. One way to view the post-1959 programs would be to treat them as part of a new development or stage in Chinese economic policy. The economic reforms introduced after 1959, however, were really nothing more than a reintroduction and continuation of the modifications of the Soviet model which the technologists had been implementing back in

1956 and 1957. Franz Schurmann reaches this same conclusion in his *Ideology and Organization in Communist
China.*

In agriculture, private plots and free markets were re-
established, and the production team—equivalent to the
lower-level agricultural producer's cooperative—was re-
established as the basic decision-making and accounting
unit. In industry, the decentralization or granting of
greater freedom of action to individual enterprise and
the introduction of greater flexibility in planning which
were discussed and partially introduced in 1956 and 1957
also were reinstated in the early 1960s.

Planning

As far as planning is concerned, the major proposals for
decentralization, greater freedom of action, and more
flexibility were all presented in an article published in
September of 1957 by Hsueh Mu-chiao, then Chairman
of the State Statistical Bureau. Hsueh had advocated that
central economic agencies should retain planning responsibility for only a few vital products and the ministries
and lower-level governments should control only those
other products which were important to the production
programs of these particular administrative agencies.
Production planning for all other products should be determined by the individual enterprises according to supply and demand. Interenterprise contracts, negotiated
under the auspices of the Ministry of Commerce, should
replace the centralized allocation of resources, which was
a major feature of the Soviet model.

Hsueh's proposals were actually implemented in the
directive on the reform of the planning system, promul-

gated jointly by the Central Committee of the Party and the State Council in September 1958, which restricted centralized planning to major products, investment, interprovince trade of major products, foreign trade, the national budget, the aggregate education plan, the aggregate allocation of labor and wages, railway transportation, and technology in state enterprises under the central government. I have been unable to find explicit verification in current Chinese publications, but I believe Hsueh's proposals represent the economic administration of planning that prevails in China today.

If this is true, then the word planning as it is used in China today does not mean what it did in the early 1950s. Rather, as is true of their colleagues in the European bloc, the technologists in China have modified their strategy of economic development to the point where it can no longer be described as the centralized allocation of resources under a plan based on nationwide material balances. On the other hand, although there are reports of proposals for the introduction of household management in agriculture, I find no substantial evidence to suggest the Chinese technologists favor the total abandonment of planning, which is now defined as a mixture of centralized and decentralized planning in key sectors or of key commodities and resources, for the allocation of commodities and resources according to profits and market prices alone.

The continuation of the reforms begun in the mid-1950s after the failure of the Great Leap Forward, of course, did not go unchallenged. Just as the advocates of the economic reforms which have done much to dismantle the Soviet model in the countries of the European bloc had literally to overthrow the followers of Stalin, the technologists in China are currently engaged in an open clash with the followers of Mao. While these two groups achieved a workable compromise in determining policy changes before the mid-1960s, they have found it impossible to do so in recent years.

The open break began at the Tenth Plenum in September 1962, which exonerated the Great Leap strategy for the long-run development of the economy. Instead the cadres were blamed for its improper implementation. While the Tenth Plenum did not reject the program of the technologists as the correct policy for achieving a revival of the economy, it did call for a renewal of the class struggle to eradicate the new class structure which was emerging due to the economic reforms of the technologists. Following the Plenum, there was contradiction, not compromise. Having experienced the damage done to the economy by the radical ideologists in 1958, the technologists could not be blamed for being unenthusiastic about another Great Leap and class struggle campaign.

Challenged by "many persons in authority" and unable to prevent the continuation and further implementation of the technologists' economic policies, an open struggle for power began in May 1966 with a wall poster campaign attacking literary and cultural personnel. It entered the political arena with the dismissal of Peng Chen and several members of the Peking Party Committee in June, and received the full support and stamp of approval from the Eleventh, or "packed," Plenum in August. This power struggle, which continues to this day, includes many more elements than the debate over economic policy alone, but the outcome of the Cultural Revolution will influence Chinese economic development policy for some time to come.

Prospects for Economic Development

Taking the last two decades as a whole, no major breakthrough into sustained economic growth was achieved,
although there was some progress in the accumulation of
physical capital and technical skills. If we use the tests
of efficiency and productivity as success indicators, China
is an underdeveloped country with a still unrealized potential for development. If we use the test of distribution
rather than production as a success indicator, however,
the Chinese have achieved a significant breakthrough.
The distribution of income has not only been made much
more equitable than in the past, but China has weathered
twenty years without a major famine. During the agricultural crisis it was touch and go, but they did not starve
to death.

As a Western-trained economist, I believe the technologists' program or approach appreciates the technical problems of economic development. Their reforms of the economic system in the early 1960s offered a possible solution
to those problems. On the other hand, as Professor Riskin
has pointed out, the Maoists are not "necessarily economic
incompetents or hopelessly impractical guerrilla idealists."
A major reason why we Western-trained economists fail
to appreciate the Maoist economic program is because
it seeks primarily to achieve political and sociological, not
economic, goals, or attempts to use political and sociological means to achieve economic goals.

Having admitted the Maoists as bona fide colleagues,
I do not believe their program will solve China's economic
development problems. This is not because Mao rejects
the free market solution, but because his program rejects

material rewards and incentives directly related to technical ability and contribution to output. It is immaterial whether the output itself is valued by a price determined on a free market, by planners, bureaucrats, or by Mao himself. Mao, of course, knows that such a system of material incentives reduces the short-run attainable rate of growth, creates classes, and prevents or postpones the realization of his sociological and political goals. He has sought to prevent this result by continual class warfare. I may fail to appreciate the need for special skills to appraise a sociological problem, but I believe Mao's program is bad sociology as well as bad economics.

The Economics of Maoism

Jack Gray

The Cultural Revolution was explicitly about cultural change, but it took the form of a struggle for political power. The policy implications generally were less prominent than the struggle itself, and among these the implications for economic policy made a relatively late entry.

Mao Tse-tung's ideas, moreover, and the manner in which he expresses them, tend to obscure the economic implications of his theory and of the practice which springs from it. "Politics takes command" seems at first sight a denial of the primacy of economic growth. "A great spiritual force can be turned into a great material force" seems to be an un-Marxist insistence on the possibility of transcending by political and ideological means the constraints of economic facts and economic laws. Mao's recent attacks on "material incentives" seem to Westerners a rejection of the most obvious and powerful means of stimulating economic enterprise. It is this sort of epigrammatic expression of the decisive importance of "ideological revolution" which has led to the Soviet denunciation of Mao Tse-tung as a voluntarist, an anti-Marxist who believes that the human will, by some magic, can wish away objective facts, and the Soviet charge has been taken up and elaborated in the West.

It may be that Mao Tse-tung's prescriptions for economic and social change have little in them that is immediately recognizable as "economics," but the record of the Cultural Revolution itself leaves little doubt of the importance of economic policy within it. The movement which led to the Great Proletarian Cultural Revolution began with the communiqué of the Tenth Plenum of the Eighth Central Committee, September 1962, which, as far as internal affairs are concerned, dealt almost entirely with economic policy. The two great models of Maoist organization, carefully nurtured since then and widely publicized, were both economic enterprises, one industrial (the Ta Ching oil field) and the other agricultural (the Tachai Production Brigade). From 1963 until 1965 there were growing signs, behind the ideological exhortations which filled the press, that the real preoccupations were with economic organization.

In August 1966, on the eve of the first great Red Guard parades, the Central Committee produced its Sixteen Point Directive for the guidance of the Cultural Revolution. This document simply dealt with the organization of the movement and had nothing whatever to say about its policy implications. The Kwangtung Provincial Committee of the Party immediately produced a long commentary upon it, interpreting its implications wholly in terms of economic organization and policy. It is even possible that the political struggle which began in April 1966 was finally touched off, not by Peng Chen's protection of liberal Party writers in Peking, but by his attempt to suppress Mao's instructions on the question of agricultural mechanization.

Finally, since the successful formation of the "three-way alliance" in 1967, which brought the main struggle to an end, the fundamental disagreements between Mao and his opponents have been spelled out in considerable detail. In the last analysis they are primarily all questions of economic policy, and it is plain that Mao's ideas on economic organization are now being very generally applied.

There can be no doubt of Mao's preoccupation in recent years with problems of economic growth, therefore, and there is no obvious case for asserting that he is primarily interested in politics and ideology. It might still be true, of course, that his interpretation of the conditions necessary for successful economic growth neglected economic analysis. It is certainly true that there is nowhere in his works any detailed attention given to problems of costs, the precise definition of effective incentives, and the alternative use of resources. And it is certainly not a sufficient explanation of his sketchy treatment of such themes to say that he leaves them to the technical economist. It is clear that he regards them as of secondary importance in the process of economic growth in a country such as China.

Mao's Writings

To some extent Mao's apparent indifference to economic questions becomes exaggerated in Western minds because attention has so far been unduly concentrated upon his writings before 1949, conveniently translated in the four volumes of his *Selected Works*. Other parts of Mao's writing, especially of his writing since 1949, have been neglected, including almost everything of economic relevance. His detailed analysis of the Border Region economy between 1940 and 1943 has never been translated, except for its preface. The *High Tide of Socialism in the Chinese Countryside*, 1956, which in three stout volumes of examples and commentary puts forward every idea of economic and social organization, later to be developed in the Commune movement and in the Cultural Revolution, has never been fully analyzed and is usually ignored. The economic implications of Mao's 1957 pamphlet *On the Correct Handling of Contradictions among the People*, developed in a wealth of exegesis, have never been dealt with because of the strange Western assumption that it dealt primarily with conflicts of opinion, while in fact (like any Marxist) Mao was actually preoccupied with conflicts of interest, and therefore with what are fundamentally economic questions.

It is not possible to elaborate here on Mao's economic ideas, but before considering the economic implications of the Cultural Revolution, it may help to put forward a hypothesis concerning them which may assist the reader in understanding what follows.

An examination of Mao's writings suggests three points of importance in the economic sphere:

1. Mao has always insisted that the emphasis of work in economics and in public finance must be on the increase of production. Taxation and state procurement must be subordinated to and dependent upon increased production. In this, he is not simply making moral noises, but reacting strongly against the static, tax-collecting tradition of Chinese administration (both traditional and Nationalist), against the counterproductive procurement policies of Stalin, and against the strong tendency of the cadres to inherit the worst of both.

2. He has always attached very great importance to material incentives in economic policy. In the perpetual tension throughout the history of Chinese Communist administration since 1927, between economic rationality

and doctrine or between economic rationality and social justice, Mao has usually been on the side of economic rationality, insisting that economic and social policies could not hope to succeed unless they were successful in raising personal incomes.

3. He has always emphasized the importance of entrepreneurship at least as strongly as any economist working on the problems of India or of Latin America. This is obscured for the Western reader only by the fact that in the West, "entrepreneur" implies an individual operating in more or less free market conditions. Mao's entrepreneurs are collectives, or more precisely individuals working through collectives. In spite of this, he meets the Western economist in the value which he attaches to willingness to innovate, willingness to take risks, and effective forethought. These are the qualities of the heroic leaders of the Tachai Production Brigade and of a thousand other economic enterprises, agricultural and industrial, which have been presented as models over the years since the "transition to socialism" and planned economic growth began in 1953. One is of course at liberty to doubt how far the collective system of China can go in producing a high level of these entrepreneurial qualities; but there can be no doubt that maximizing these qualities within that system is one of Mao's preoccupations—perhaps his greatest and most constant preoccupation in the economic field.

In order to see how far these considerations have influenced the course and the consequences of the Cultural Revolution, one must evade as far as possible the general statements made by Mao and his supporters, and look at the problem in a concrete form. Mao addresses himself to the grass-roots: to half-educated sons of workers and peasants, to subliterate lower-level cadres, and to the still largely illiterate masses. He is therefore more concerned to express himself in memorable slogans than in statistical tables. The slogans provide texts which his local supporters then elaborate in concrete terms, largely by verbal communication. This present study is deliberately based largely upon publications in Chinese specialist journals, where one might expect that Mao's case would be put in its most sophisticated form; but even there, especially as the Cultural Revolution gathered strength, the slogan, the epigram, and the mnemonic soon came to dominate what was published. It is only by taking one important practical issue and examining it that one can bring Maoist economics down to reality.

Tenth Plenum Policy

One key issue in the struggle which was developing over economic policy and organization after 1962 was the question of the best means to achieve the mechanization of Chinese agriculture. The Communiqué of the Tenth Plenum put forward a new economic policy expressed in the formula: "Take agriculture as the foundation of the economy, and industry as the leading factor." This was a reaction to the agricultural disasters of the preceding three years. It looked forward not simply to giving agriculture priority in economic planning, and to the fullest possible use of industry to equip agriculture, but also to two specific policies: first, the transformation of agricultural technology by the development of mechanization, electrification, water conservancy, and the use of chemical fertilizers; and second, concentration upon the creation of areas of stable high yields as a defense against the natural disasters which had so damaged the economy between 1959 and 1961.

In relation to this, the Tenth Plenum reasserted much more strongly than any previous statement the idea that class struggle must be expected to continue after the foundation of the socialist state. The context showed, and subsequent comments confirmed, that renewed class struggle was closely related to the new policy of transforming agricultural technology. The full resources of the collectives would have to be mobilized for investment in agriculture if the new plans were to be realized; the diversion of savings and labor into the private sector which had been permitted to flourish increasingly since 1959 would have to be curtailed.

Behind this decision by the Central Committee lay two issues which might (in spite of the resounding phrases in which this new consensus was expressed) give grounds for renewed and fundamental disagreement. First, it is very probable that the reassertion of collectivist agriculture was not accepted with equal wholeheartedness by all the leaders. The form (the small cooperative represented by the production team, or the very large collective represented by the Commune?) was not defined, nor was the degree to which the private sector would be reduced. Second, nothing was said about how collective resources would be mobilized: in the form of local savings directly invested by the collective as in the Communes of 1958; or by increased taxation and procurement making possible greater central investment in agriculture by the state?

Tractors and Peasants

In relation to the new economic policy, the question of agricultural mechanization and how it could be achieved was of fundamental importance. The crux of agricultural mechanization is the tractor. In 1952-53, the first tractor stations appeared in China. They were operated by the state and fees charged for their services to the farmers. That some of China's leaders were unhappy from the beginning about this acceptance in China of the Soviet organization of agricultural mechanization is now revealed by quotations from remarks reported to have been made by Kang Sheng (now one of the hard-core Maoist group) in 1954 after his return from a tour of inspection of the Soviet Union:

"Collective farms in the Soviet Union have many machines, but output is nevertheless low, and costs are high. . . ." And on the Chinese imitation of the Soviet Union's tractor stations: "This is the problem that must be solved: how to link the tractors to the peasants. . . . If tractor stations continue to be run in their present form . . . they will become disguised tax-collectors, and will hold the peasants to ransom, as the Soviet tractor stations do. . . ."

Consequently, when collectivization had been rapidly completed in 1956 under pressure from Mao Tse-tung, backed by a conference representing not only the Party leadership but the provincial, municipal, and regional authorities throughout China, experiments were conducted in Manchuria and in North China in permitting the collectives to run their own tractors. In March 1958 (we are now informed by Red Guard sources) at a conference at Chengtu in Szechuan, Mao Tse-tung advocated that agricultural mechanization should be carried out through the collectives themselves, buying the equipment out of their own resources and operating it on their own account. Although this decision was apparently suppressed by the Party's right wing, when the Communes were formed later in the same year, seventy per cent of the existing tractors were handed over to them.

The opposition, however, displayed their lack of enthusiasm by carrying this out in a perfunctory way, giving no help or guidance to the Communes: "In some places a meeting was held in the morning, and the tractors were driven away in the afternoon." For two years, say Mao's supporters, the relevant ministries did not hand down a single document nor convene a single conference to assist the Communes in handling the machinery. The Communes suffered heavy losses, and those who supported the alternative policy of providing mechanization through the state were then able to argue that the experiment had been a costly failure, not only for the Communes themselves but for the state, which had to bail them out.

This Maoist story implies that the opposition was basically indifferent to mechanization of agriculture. Liu Shao-chi and Po I-po are quoted to prove this, but the quotations are obviously torn from their context and almost certainly misrepresent their views on the desirability of mechanization, as opposed to the methods of achieving it. The Maoists can nevertheless point to the fact that the business of agricultural mechanization was split among three different ministries, and generally bandied about from hand to hand in a way which does not suggest that the Liu Shao-chi administration gave the problem very high priority. Local tractor and equipment plants were apparently closed down and much of the industry made subordinate to the production of other types of motor vehicles.

Communal Mechanization

The recommendation of the Chengtu Conference of March
1958 that the collectives themselves should take the initiative in mechanization was, it is claimed, suppressed
until "some people discovered it" in 1965. Mao's only
victory in this issue was to secure in 1963 the establishment of a Ministry in whole and sole charge of agricultural mechanization, a measure which he had sought
since 1956. It was, however, short-lived, and was per-
verted from its intended purpose of providing guidance
to communal mechanization, into the centralized manufacture of equipment within the system of state operation then being evolved by Liu Shao-chi and Peng Chen.
This was a centralized and monopolistic system, culminating in 1965 in a proposal to change the various economic
ministries into trusts, of which the China Tractor and
Internal Combustion Company was one. They hoped
eventually that these public trusts would operate directly
under the state Economic Commission, outside the control of the Party committees at all levels, and outside the
control of local government bodies, and that the operations of these trusts would be judged by their profitability.

As far as the problem of agricultural mechanization is
concerned, the crisis came in early 1966. Mao Tse-tung
(Red Guard sources state) took up a report on the problem prepared by the Hupeh Provincial Committee, a report favorable to his own views, and requested that it be
given nationwide Party circulation. Liu Shao-chi refused
to circulate the report, or Mao's accompanying comments,
until the Central Committee had given its opinion. He
gave Peng Chen the task of drafting this opinion. Peng

Chen did so, and he also edited Mao's own comments, cutting out Mao's warnings against rigid centralization, and also (which was both significant and infuriating) cut out his condemnation of Soviet agricultural policy. Within days, Lin Piao's troops turned Peng Chen out of his office, and the Cultural Revolution became a struggle for political power.

Intermediate Technology

A subsidiary issue was the fate of Mao's attempt to organize and guide the peasants to develop their own "intermediate technology" by systematic improvement of existing tools. In 1958, he had called for research stations in every province. In 1959, he put forward a plan for units in every *hsien*, in which scientists, technicians, local blacksmiths, and carpenters would be associated with veteran farmers in working out new tools suitable to their locality. The Liu faction took no interest in this, believing that such an intermediate technology could at best have only a temporary importance, and they persisted more and more in pursuing "bigness, modernity, completeness, and newness."

We have, of course, only the Maoist story of these events. Although a rapid check back through the documentation of the years in question certainly shows that a muted struggle on these lines was going on, we have no access to any full statement of the opposition's case. We have to work, for the present, with what the Maoists chose to quote of it in the course of their attacks. If these quotations (which are very repetitive and sometimes contradictory) are organized into something as near to logic as they will permit, the argument is broadly as follows:

Since the peasants are unable to do the job, the State must do
it. Although ownership and operation by the Commune has
been implemented, actually investment is still made by the
State, and operational losses are still subsidized by the State.
We must equip whole *hsien* one by one. Many machines must
be concentrated in one *hsien*. In ten years the State will invest
a very large sum of money, and it will begin to recover it at the
end of these ten years. The State will then use this sum of
money to equip another area. The State will have to invest ten
to twenty billion *yuan*.

In charging fees [for the use of tractors] fields should be
divided into a number of grades. The fees charged may be
lower for large plots and higher for small plots. Operations
should be guided by price.

The power of the trust (in capitalist countries) is very great.
The capitalist experience of management of enterprises—especially of monopolistic enterprises—should be studied. The
bureaus of the various ministries are to be converted into companies and become, not administrative organizations, but enterprises. Let us set up a trust [for agricultural machinery] and
set up supply stations along railway lines and highways. We
should not set up stations according to administrative divisions,
nor should we make direct allocations to the *hsien*. All stations
should be run independently of the local governments.

Our present method is for provinces, municipalities, regions,
and the different departments of the Central Committee to
interfere with the economy. This is an extra-economic method.
It is not a capitalist method, but a feudal method.

It is clear that the "Party people in authority taking the
capitalist road" were in fact, on this vital issue as well as
in many others, taking the road of East European liberali-
zation. Before we assume, however, that because Liu Shao-
chi seems to be a liberal in this sense, Mao must represent
resurgent Stalinism, it may be as well to quote Mao Tse-
tung's opinion of Soviet agriculture, written in his comments on the 1966 Hupeh proposals, and edited out by
the liberals: "The agricultural policy of the Soviet Union

has always been wrong in that *it drains the pond to catch the fish,* and is divorced from the masses, thus resulting in the present dilemma."

This, it may be noted, is more than an attack on "Khrushchev revisionism." Soviet agricultural policy has *"always been wrong,"* and its failing—ruthless procurement—is one which Mao and his audience know very well was at its unbelievable worst not under Stalin's successors but under Stalin himself.

Mao Versus Liu

The Maoist arguments against Liu Shao-chi's policy on agricultural mechanization, put into a connected argument, are as follows:

The cause of agricultural mechanization must be made to establish flesh-and-blood ties with the masses. We always advocate that revolution depends on the masses of the people and on everybody going into action, and are opposed to depending on a few people issuing orders. We should bring local initiative more into play and, under the unified planning of the central government, let the localities do more.

Collectives must depend on their own strength to achieve agricultural mechanization. Mechanization should be linked with defense and famine and should serve the people. Reliance on State investment would be "draining the pond to catch the fish," reflecting the mistakes of Soviet revisionism. State operation of tractor stations makes it impossible for the peasants generally to grasp modern production methods and technical knowledge. In this way the difference between workers and peasants will widen and widen. The tractor stations obliged to show a profit have refused to plough for communes and teams in difficulties.

If the monopolistic agricultural machinery trust merely considers specialization in and standardization of a few products without giving any consideration to the actual needs of the rural communes—especially the areas with low output and poor communications—in what way is it different from the capitalists who "have only an eye for gain" and "refuse to do unprofitable business"?

Disparate Views

Thus two distinct economic points of view emerge on this issue. The Liu administration seeks to get rid of political and administrative interference in economic organization; to improve efficiency by concentrating production, cutting out small inefficient enterprises, and standardizing products; to avoid wasteful investment by putting the operation of the industry on the clear and simple basis of profit and loss; to avoid wasteful use of resources by keeping the operation and repair, as well as the manufacture, of agricultural equipment in skilled hands. The means they chose to apply were those which were at the same time being experimented with in other Communist countries at much the same time.

The Maoist view, however, emphasizes the following points:

1. The peasants will not take an interest in mechanization or try to exploit its possibilities fully unless and until they have the machines at their own disposal, so that they can "regard the machines as a dependable force for the all-round development of production in a planned manner," instead of regarding them as something foreign which they call on, if at all, only when hard-pressed in the busy season. The idea that tractor stations themselves should take responsibility for directing local agricultural production is emphatically rejected.

2. Reliance on state investment for mechanization would mean, in one form or another, increased procurement of agricultural produce to pay for mechanization, through centralized institutions remote from the peasants. It would "drain the pond to catch the fish."

3. State operation of equipment provides no "educational fallout."

4. Centralized monopoly of the industry deprives the local communities of one of their most obvious lines of industrial growth: service to local agriculture. This and the previous point are combined in the statement that the movement for the improvement of farm tools which Mao sought to maintain "promoted local industry and handicrafts and also helped people to free their minds from superstitious attitudes and dogmatism about agricultural mechanization."

5. Using profit as the criterion of efficiency in the operation of agricultural machinery stations will tend to concentrate development in the richer areas and leave the poorer and remoter areas untouched, thus widening the gap (already politically important) between the richer and the poorer areas of China.

6. The dependence of the peasants on mechanization provided by skilled technicians and workers from outside would widen the existing social gulf between urban workers and rural peasants.

To sum up these points, Mao is opposed to the monopolization of agricultural machinery by the state on the grounds that it would increase the state's procurement needs and add to the peasants' burden; that it would impoverish the development of the local economies by minimizing the opportunities of the peasant communities to master modern technology and to develop local industry; and that it would tend to increase rather than diminish two existing social gulfs—that between city

workers and the rural farming population, and that between the richer and poorer parts of China.

Of these points, clearly the most important in his mind
is the question of education through participation. "The
important question is the education of the peasants," is
one of Mao's most frequently quoted aphorisms. Applied
to the question of agricultural mechanization, it means
that the peasants will not accept, or fully use, *or pay for*,
agricultural mechanization unless they can be brought
to appreciate its full possibilities in the amelioration of
their own lives. It also means that this appreciation will
be developed only by inducing the villagers gradually,
through their own efforts toward an intermediate technology, to mechanize out of their own resources and to
operate the machines with their own hands, in a milieu
in which local industry, agricultural mechanization, agricultural diversification, and the education (both formal
and informal) growing out of these activities mutually
enrich each other.

Perhaps the key to Mao's convictions is best provided
by an account given in the *Draft History of Agricultural
Taxes* of a controversy which is said to have taken place
among the Party leaders during the discussions following
the end of the First Five-Year Plan. Agricultural production and incomes had increased during the first plan. The
question was whether or not procurement assessments
should therefore be increased in the second plan. Such an
increase would have been orthodox communist practice,
on the assumption that any increased investment made
possible by the increase in production should be made
centrally by the state. According to the *Draft History*,
written explicitly as concrete illustration of Mao's discussion of conflicts of interest among individual, collective, and state in his pamphlet *On the Correct Handling*

of Contradictions among the People, Mao insisted that
the absolute quantity of taxes and compulsory purchases
should remain the same, and the surplus accruing from
increased production should be left in the hands of the
collectives, to be invested by the collectives themselves.

The reason which Mao is said to have advanced for
this unorthodox policy was that the peasants would learn
to appreciate the nature of the relationships among individual, collective, and state interests—and the crux of this
was an appreciation of what industry could do for them—
only if they developed and operated industry for themselves. He had already made it clear in his own pamphlet
that he regarded the state bureaucracy as the biggest
obstacle to the growth of an appreciation among the population generally of the basic identity of individual and
communal interests which the Party's economic planning
was supposed to enshrine.

This was the basic argument behind the Great Leap
Forward and the Communes, and the examination made
here of the problems of agricultural mechanization shows
that, for Mao, the argument still stands.

Parallels in the West

Significantly, while Mao has been working out the implications of his ideas on the "education of the peasant"
as the fundamental problem of the Chinese economy,
Western economists have been coming to parallel conclusions. In the decade since the Communes were established, it has become a commonplace in the West to say
that the problems of economic growth in poor countries
are very often not, in any obvious sense, economic prob-

lems at all, but are problems of ignorance and apathy, and of social habits and attitudes in the underdeveloped countries.

We do not deny to men who emphasize this idea the title of economists, and there is no reason why we should believe that Mao's ideas, however idiosyncratic, indicate that he has no thoughts on economics. Indeed, once the similarity of his ideas to our own is recognized, we should acknowledge that he was the first to express them. Having done so, we may understand his ideas better by noting that he is the only statesman anywhere who has made a determined and intelligible effort to transcend the "contradiction" between economic incentives on the one hand, and fear and ignorance on the other, by policies which seek to maximize the educational effects of participation in production.

These ideas of Mao Tse-tung, expressing a concern with material incentives, a rational procurement system, and a preoccupation with the development of entrepreneurial qualities, are obscured by his insistence on a high level of collectivism. Western views of what collectivism is and how it works are, of course, based on the depressing history of Soviet collective agriculture in the Soviet Union itself and in the East European Communist countries. It is impossible to discuss Mao's economic ideas and policies intelligibly if one assumes from this history that Soviet and East European agriculture has failed simply because it is collective. There is no warrant for such a conclusion.

In the story of the failure of Soviet-type agriculture, the mere fact of collective organization is probably the least of it. Uneconomic levels of procurement, starvation of capital, starvation of talent, lack of consumer goods, direction from outside by an urban-based and urban-biased Party—almost any one of these factors is enough to account for the stagnation of agriculture. One might also add that in comparing the Russian kholkhoz with the Chinese collective (cooperatives until 1958, Communes thereafter) the totally different historical situations from which they sprang have influenced their development and their possibilities. The attitude of the Soviet Party to agriculture sprang from the pre-revolutionary situation in which, as the Russian economy broke down under the strain of war, the countryside had to be dragooned into supplying the starving towns. Collectivization in Russia was a response to emergency conditions— undertaken before the threat of famine, and forced through by civil war.

On the contrary, in China Mao Tse-tung has been able to choose his moment, and every step in the development of collective enterprise in China has been taken in the wake of economic success. The movement for the organization of agriculture was launched in 1953 when the economy had recovered from the devastation of the Japanese war. It was completed in 1956 after the bumper harvest of 1955. The Communes were set up in 1958 after the record harvests of 1957. The movement to restore the collectives after the bad years of 1959-61 began with the first normal harvest in 1962, but the Cultural Revolution was launched only after a steady improvement in agricultural production from 1962-65. If there has been an element of force in the collectivization of rural life in China, there has also been an element of optimism, derived from successful experience. There has also been the long experience of the Chinese Communist Party during the Kiangsi Soviet and the Japanese war of running a rural economy in conditions which enforced even at the outset and without institutional change a significant level of cooperative activity on the part of the rural population.

Reaction against Soviet Model

It is thus possible to approach Mao's collectivist ideas and policies in a questioning, rather than a dogmatic, spirit, and to judge them on their merits. They may then be seen to represent a reaction against the Soviet model at almost every point.

The first and perhaps the most important contrast to be made concerns procurement. On this there does not appear to be much dispute in China. While the *étatist* policies of the Liu administration are opposed by Mao partly because they seem to imply an increase in procurement, it is notable that throughout the period during which the controversies have been going on, with the means of publicity at first firmly in the hands of Liu's administration and then in the hands of the Maoists, past levels of procurement are not an issue. Even at times when the most liberalizing elements in China have been able to make their voices heard, this has remained true. (This tends to confirm work done in the West on the subject.) Even those who advocated between 1959 and 1961 that the family and not the collective should be assessed for taxation and state purchases did not go on to argue that the burden ought to be lightened. It seems to be accepted in China that procurement prices, even if they are inevitably below free market prices, cover production costs and leave a profit. The Chinese have not "drained the pond to catch the fish."

As far as capital for agricultural development is concerned, we have seen evidence that Mao Tse-tung prefers to encourage the collectives to invest for themselves rather than increase state investment. The funds for such investment are expected to come from increased production of agricultural produce and—not least—from successful diversification of the local economy through handicrafts, animal husbandry, and afforestation, according to the possibilities of the area. Such diversification has played an important part in increasing local capital accumulation since the very beginning of the organization of agriculture in 1953.

As far as talent is concerned, and this as we have seen is to Mao the most fundamental point, he believes in diversification, work-study education, a drive for the spread of scientific attitudes through the "democratization" of science, and—at a level nearer to coercive measures— the sending of educated youth in enormous numbers down to the villages to make their lives there. In general the maximization of education opportunities, with this in mind, will prevent the villages from being drained of talent and enterprise, and will develop latent talent to the fullest extent.

The implications of all this are that the collectives will be run by peasant cadres for the peasants, and not dominated, as in the Soviet Union, by urban bureaucrats and technicians.

Finally, Mao seeks to avoid the Soviet problem that lack of consumer goods leads to lack of incentive to market agricultural produce by encouraging local economic diversification.

These are the features of the system of cooperative production which Mao seeks to develop. He may not be right, but it would be difficult to argue that he is irrational. The only argument which could prove his ideas irrational would be the argument that collective incentives, through the shared profits of cooperative working, must in all circumstances prove ineffective.

Class Struggle

The question remains, however, that if Mao Tse-tung
puts forward this essentially economic argument, based
upon incentives and how to make these incentives effective by education, why then does he feel obliged to justify
his policies by non-economic slogans such as "Let politics
take command," and why does he feel obliged to emphasize that a class struggle is involved?

There are two quite distinct phenomena involved in
what Mao now characterizes as class struggle, and although neither of them is class struggle in the classical
Marxist sense, they certainly represent certain Chinese
social realities.

The first phenomenon is the crystallization in China after
the revolution of a "new class" in the sense in which this
phrase has been used by Djilas, composed of Party administrators, managers, and technicians. There is a wealth
of evidence (from first-hand observers in China) of
mandarin-like behavior by cadres, of privileged schools
for the sons of cadres, and all the other depressingly predictable signs of the formation of a new and hereditary
ruling class perpetuating many of the attitudes of their
predecessors. This is the fundamental point of Mao's resistance to the extention of state enterprise. It is a political and social point rather than economic, but Mao draws
from it the economic lesson that if such a ruling group
hardens out, it will put an insuperable obstacle in the way
of the development of the abilities and sense of responsibility of the mass of the population on which economic
vigor in the last analysis depends.

Halting the Drain

The second phenomenon is that within the collectives some individuals (whom Mao believes to be a small minority) have the means to participate profitably in the private sector and the free market which grew rapidly after 1959. It is obvious that at Chinese standards of income and saving, collective enterprise is unlikely to succeed without the participation of the more prosperous and the more skilled. Their concentration upon individual enterprise and private profit is therefore a mortal drain on collective resources, and must be stopped. His condemnation of Soviet procurement policy can be assumed to have the corollary that the private sector in the Soviet Union was a necessity of life when the whole economy was organized on the basis of exploiting the collective to the point where collective agricultural operations were carried on at a steady loss and maintained by sheer force. Clearly if Mao's concept of the collective was successfully applied, there would be no such necessity in China. The limitation and eventually the elimination of the private sector he therefore regards as both necessary and justified. "Class struggle" in the countryside is directed at removing this obstacle to collective investment and enterprise.

To prevent the growth of these two social phenomena, the new class of technocrats and the new class of private-sector operators, politics must take command. If these new cleavages in Chinese society are prevented, and the ring held for the development of collective entrepreneurship, then Mao believes that "a great spiritual force will be transformed into a great material force": the masses of China will at last become aware of the infinite possibilities of material progress through modern technology and large-scale social organization, and will launch a massive war for the control and exploitation of nature, before which they have lived precariously throughout history. In the light of Mao Tse-tung's explicit policies, it is unnecessary to see in such slogans an excessive faith in the human will, or a romantic preoccupation with struggle for its own sake. Nor are they simply an expression of his own personality. The Chinese people may rise massively to the occasion, or they may not, but to expect them to do so is not excessively romantic.

The Evidence

There exists, moreover, evidence of a sort by which Mao Tse-tung seeks to prove that he is right. It consists of the description of the experience and achievements of individual collectives. A constant stream of such descriptions has poured out since 1953. As each case gives time, place, and individual names, and as in most cases the collective concerned was opened to public view as an example and seen by hundreds and in some instances thousands of peasants, it can be assumed that the descriptions do not depart too far from reality.

Taken as a whole, these exemplary cooperatives, Communes, production brigades, or production teams cannot of course provide any guide to average performance nor were they intended to provide this. They represent Maoist performance at its best, they represent what the rest of China might eventually achieve, and they give an enormous amount of detail about how their results were won. They have been totally neglected by specialists on

China, but no attempt to evaluate Maoism is possible without reference to them, whatever the difficulties the use of such material may involve. An analysis of this material could at least answer the question whether Maoism, in the sense discussed, exists only as an aspiration, or has reality at least here and there in China.

It is clear, however, that a Maoist economic system cannot exist only in spots. Mao's economic program involves the integration of all economic activity in China, as well as the provision of a national political framework to support the program in its first stages. During the Cultural Revolution, during which he had been careful to reveal his hand only gradually as the struggle deepened and widened to take in larger and larger sectors of Chinese society, he had nowhere stated systematically what economic policy and organization would be. But there exists one document which can illustrate many aspects of the future. This is the Report of the Kwangtung Provincial Committee of August 1966, in which the Maoists of South China set forth their interpretation of the meaning of the Cultural Revolution. It was never acknowledged by the Peking Maoist leadership. It represents an extreme view, and its publication over the provincial radio may indeed have played a part in the condemnation of Tao Chu, the most important southern leader in the early stages of the Cultural Revolution, on charges which included "ultra-leftism." If it was opposed, however, it must have been more on grounds of its call for full, immediate and therefore coercive implementation of the Maoist line than because it misrepresented the final implications of the line. The passages relevant to economic organization can be summarized as follows:

Chairman Mao's instruction exhibits to us a magnificent blueprint of communism, points out the concrete road to the elimination of the three great differences and the transition to com-

munism. Previously, we always thought that the scientific prediction of Marx and Engels on the elimination of the three
great differences was a matter of the distant future. Having
studied this instruction of Chairman Mao, we feel that it is
already on our agenda, and something quite tangible.

The most fundamental measure is to turn the whole province
into a big school for the study of Mao Tse-tung's thinking.
Workers, peasants, soldiers, students, and commercial circles,
and all sectors of the economy, must, in their own work posts,
take an active part in class struggle, in the socialist education
campaign, and in the great proletarian Cultural Revolution, and
criticize the bourgeoisie. Meanwhile they should also learn
politics, military affairs, and culture, becoming truly worker-
peasants wielding both pen and sword.

All enterprises with suitable conditions should introduce in a
big way the worker-peasant labor system, particularly enterprises with close relations with agriculture. Existing enterprises
and those built or extended in future should, in the light of
the characteristics of their trade, respectively adopt the system
of rotation workers, temporary workers, seasonal workers, or
contracted workers with the Communes and brigades, and
gradually turn a number of permanent workers into worker-
peasants. In a methodical manner, remove some factories to
the rural areas, particularly the existing processing industry
which depends on farm and sideline products as raw materials.
These should either set up processing centers or actively develop the processing industry within the collective economy.
All factories, mines, and enterprises with suitable conditions
should engage in farm and sideline production. They should
actively integrate the factory with the Communes, having the
factory lead the Commune, etc., on a trial basis, thus integrating industry with agriculture.

Commercial points and networks in rural areas should hand
over some of their work to the rural Communes, brigades, and
production teams. The basic-level finance and trade units
should put into effect the system of rotation workers who will
be recommended by the collective. These will include workers
for commerce, food, supply and marketing, finance and tax-

collection, banking, and the granting of loans. All small business and peddling in basic-level commerce in the countryside of the province must be thoroughly reformed.

In future the development of state-run farming, forestry, and reclamation must follow the line of joint management by the State and the Commune. Existing state-run farms, forestry and reclamation farms must also at the same time be people's Communes. All agricultural forestry and reclamation farms must diversify their economy, with agriculture as the main pursuit.

In accordance with the characteristics of the Communes which are big and public, the Communes should step by step develop into basic level organizations with agriculture as the main pursuit and at the same time running industry and wielding pen and sword. They should, with agriculture as the main pursuit, run one or two major industrial and sideline productions in the light of local conditions; with food grain as the main crop, they should grow one or two major industrial crops. In the light of local conditions, step by step set up small farms, small forestry farms, agricultural science centers and agricultural machinery stations. Actively and methodically develop Commune industry, handicraft industry and joint management of industry and handicrafts by Commune and brigade. Every year the Communes must spontaneously and methodically send peasants to factories to be rotation workers, seasonal workers, or temporary workers; to join the Army; to attend various schools or training courses; to be "political apprentices," to take part in various political campaigns, etc.

The leadership of the schools must be truly in the hands of the proletariat. . . . Reform the education system of schools, resolutely implementing the principles of education serving proletarian politics and education integrating with productive labor. . . . All-day schools must be methodically and gradually transformed into work-farmwork-study schools. Schools built in future must be located in the countryside without exception. . . . Students should come from the Communes and go back to them, and be fostered into new-type laborers that combine mental and manual labor.

The superstructure must serve better the economic basis. Structures should be resolutely streamlined, sweeping away all ideas, viewpoints, regulations and systems that are unfavorable to the diminishing of the three great differences. . . . Office cadres must go deep into the basic levels to stay at points, strengthen the mass viewpoint, and make a success of investigations and study. Cadres must particularly be made to take part in productive labor.

It is perhaps in the idea of the "destruction of the three great differences"—among industry and agriculture, town and country, and mental and manual labor—that Mao's point of view on social and economic change is best summed up. In Karl Marx's own writings, the elimination of these social gulfs was expected to follow the creation of communism: it was a characteristic of the final classless Utopia. In Mao's thought, their elimination becomes instead the most critical step toward successful economic development in his own underdeveloped country, a step now planned in detail.

The argument in China does not, of course, involve free enterprise as one of the choices. The alternatives at present are represented by the policies of Mao and those which he ascribes to Liu Shao-chi, both Communist and equally alien to Western ideas of economic organization. Westerners, fortunately, do not have to make the choice, but we have an interest in the results. If Mao Tse-tung's social and economic program should prove successful in solving the problems of ignorance, fear, and social disunity, which he regards as fundamental obstacles to rapid economic growth, we cannot but remember that half of the world suffers bitterly from the existence of similar obstacles, and his solution—if a solution it should prove to be—might have very wide application.

FOREIGN
POLICY

Although foreign affairs did not seem during the Cultural Revolution to claim the attention that was devoted to political, social, and economic issues, all of China's neighbors were affected by it. For a time during 1967 it looked as if a more radical Chinese leadership was abandoning the formula of coexistence which had governed relations with such neutral states as Burma, Nepal, and Cambodia, and even with the two surviving European colonies of Hong Kong and Macao. China's relationship with fellow Communist regimes in Mongolia, North Korea, and North Vietnam also suffered. But have the events of the past two or three years affected the basic posture of China toward the Soviet Union and the United States?

In the three articles that follow, the main aspects of China's international relations are considered. C. P. Fitzgerald gives a general account of foreign policy in the light of the Cultural Revolution. Richard Harris comments on Fitzgerald's presentation, with special reference to what he has called China's "Thirty Years' War" with the U.S. John Lindbeck describes which foreign links have been broken and which have survived the internal upheaval in China in terms of student, technical, and science exchanges. Michael Yahuda, a political scientist, discusses China's nuclear weapons development in the light of her diplomatic goals.

A Revolutionary Hiatus

C. P. Fitzgerald

Whether the Chinese Great Proletarian Cultural Revolution is reaching its final phase, has already virtually ended, or still holds the possibility of further developments and surprises, cannot be foreseen. One fact does seem more certain, and that is that as a result of the stresses of the Cultural Revolution in the past two years there has been a virtual hiatus in the development and implementation of foreign policy. It is very hard to show that China has taken any positive initiative during these two years, and easy to suggest that the actions and pronouncements of her Ministry for Foreign Affairs have been motivated much more by *ad hoc* responses to events in China itself than to any consistent line of policy toward the outside world.

In the summer of 1967, Red Guards, themselves at least in part recruited from the junior staff of the Foreign Ministry, occupied that institution, treated its senior officials with contempt and disdain, sent off instructions to overseas posts without the authority of the Minister or any senior official, and treated the confidential files without the least consideration for security. "What is so sacred about secrets?" reportedly commented one young

Red Guard. What, indeed? Whether foreign intelligence
services have benefited from this robust iconoclasm is not
known. It does suggest that in effect China can have no
coherent foreign policy during the reign of the Red
Guards.

This phase was ended, and the skillful leadership of
Chou En-lai reinstated the normal control in the Ministry and evicted the "rebels." In 1968, there seemed to
be cautious tentatives to mend some of the fences through
which the Red Guards rode so roughshod last year.
That the "rebel" occupation of the Ministry did great
damage to China is incontestable, and will be considered.
It is as well to reflect that even during this extraordinary
incursion, certain broad lines of foreign policy, inherited
from the period before the Cultural Revolution, were not
changed or challenged. They went on, as it were, by their
own momentum, because no one proposed anything different. Hostility to the USSR was in no way abated; nor
was criticism and denunciation of the United States. In
these matters the attitude of the Cultural Revolutionaries
does not differ at all from that formerly displayed by the
"handful of top Party members taking the capitalist road,"
or the senior policy makers in the Foreign Ministry. Liu
Shao-chi and Peng Chen are on record as having used
very strong terms in denouncing the Soviet and the U.S.
administration. Wherever the capitalist road they are alleged to have followed was going to lead them, there are
no signs that it would have conducted them to harmony
or even détente with the USSR or the United States. It is
not the countries whom China regarded as her foes who
have suffered from any changes in policy; it is those who
were formerly regarded as her friends.

Internal and External

This peculiar feature of the present upheaval may be of more significance in an assessment of the internal crisis than in an analysis of foreign policy. It tends to suggest that internal political and social issues are the real matters in dispute, and that foreign relations have been left aside or regarded as only of peripheral importance. There is certainly much to show that China has been preoccupied with her domestic crisis and that the Cultural Revolution has turned attention away from foreign questions. The emphasis on classes drawn from the less educated—and quite untraveled—sections of the nation, the downgrading of all who had "bourgeois" background, must mean that those who have exercised influence are precisely those to whom foreign countries mean very little, and relations with them are seen as only to be guided by limited and literal adherence to pure revolutionary doctrine. Even Mao Tse-tung's *Red Book of Quotations* is a guide which does not guide, for international relations is not a subject to which it pays any serious attention.

Opposition to the USSR, the stronghold of "revisionism," is a simple rule of thumb. It could not be otherwise. Denunciation of American imperialism is another dogma: the United States is the leading capitalist power, therefore those who "take the road back to capitalism" are at least suspect of heading toward it, and by a further simple inference, must be themselves likely agents for the imperialists to enlist. Old policies such as these can run on under their own steam. It does not occur to the revolutionaries that they, too, should be reassessed or modified.

More important is the question whether the Army men who now act as chairmen of almost all the new provincial revolutionary committees which have replaced the old Party leaders, and clearly must also exercise an increasing influence at the center, are so ill informed about, or so indifferent to, the national interest. It would not seem likely that this is so. The Army has for years been taught that its most probable main task will be to defend the nation against an American attack or invasion. However improbable this fear may seem outside China, it is not realistic to discount its plausibility to the Chinese people. The Army and its senior officers must of necessity have carefully considered and studied the possible occasions which could provoke or cause such an American attack, and this means that they must have studied problems of foreign relations.

The Army's Attitude

Probability is confirmed by the manner in which the Chinese armed forces have reacted, or not reacted, to various incidents which could have been used by a bellicose service to cause serious situations. Air intrusions, accidental or not so accidental, provoke strong protests, but no action. Chinese aircraft have not retaliated on the tit-for-tat basis of flying over U.S. installations in Vietnam, or at sea. Language is strong, but action is cautious. This very much suggests that the higher Army command has no intention of being led into this situation by Red Guards or anyone else. An army which is charged with the responsibility of defending a nation against the most powerful antagonist in the world, and knows that relations with that power are bad, is going to move very carefully. Time gained is precious: other, more modern armaments are in preparation, and if conflict can be postponed until they are in good supply, it may never happen at all.

The Army may not feel able, or even be willing, to moderate the violence of abuse of America. Words, after all, butter no parsnips. It would be difficult and dangerous, politically, to suggest moderation in present circumstances. But when it comes to action or inaction in response to incidents, the Army can decide for itself and needs no explanations. It is at least possible that professional soldiers, even of the People's Liberation Army, behave like their counterparts elsewhere. They pay a great deal of attention to military facts and strategic considerations, very much less to what politicians may from day to day find it necessary to declaim.

If reflex continuation of an old policy, and Army caution in carrying it out, may account for China's unchanged attitude toward America, the same factors cannot explain the policy toward the USSR. There are obvious differences. Russia is not engaged in a war close to China's borders which threatens and involves a neighboring Communist state. However evil Russian revisionism may be, or may be described as being, it is not actively engaged in attempting to crush a Communist insurgent movement. The Chinese do accuse Russia of collusion with the United States in the Vietnam war, but this far-fetched suggestion cannot be documented, nor indeed made to carry any conviction at all. It is strange collusion that provides North Vietnam with sophisticated weapons for immediate use against the U.S. Air Force. It can only be assumed that this piece of anti-Soviet propaganda is intended by the Chinese leadership for those who are too uninstructed or too occupied with other matters to follow the course of the war. China has, or perhaps formerly had, some reason to fear that escalation of the war in Vietnam could lead to an open conflict with America, but it is not at all evident that any escalation of the verbal battle with the Russians need lead to a conflict on the common borders.

The Frontiers

Those frontiers are very long and pass through country which is remote from the homelands of either Chinese or Russians. The inhabitants on both sides are often indigenous peoples—Kazaks, Khirgiz, and others—who were or still are largely nomadic herdsmen. They were accustomed to moving flocks and herds across boundaries as the weather or the state of pasturage might suggest. Such movement, in times of tension and clashing polemics, is easily described as either "the flight of an oppressed minority" or the "intrusion of hostile elements." Foreign correspondents have no access to these regions and such reports as Chinese or Russian sources put out must be held to be mainly propagandist in form and intention. These reports have mentioned increasing concentration of frontier guards and regular forces by both sides, but whether these measures are designed to stop tribal movements and at the same time to show determination to resist any incursions, or merely to keep the tribes in submission and prevent subversion, is unknown. Probably all these considerations are involved. For China the Sinkiang region is sensitive, for it is the area in which the nuclear weapons program is based, where much of the uranium is mined, and which also holds major oil fields. It would be natural enough for such a region to be strongly defended.

China has in her polemical attacks upon the USSR frequently cited the Tsarist annexations beyond the Amur

River and also in northwest Sinkiang. The fact that the
USSR continues to enjoy the fruits of these encroachments, and has never shown any overt sign of repentance
or restitution, gives the Chinese a neat propaganda point.
Is this the behavior of a socialist state? Those who profit
from the acts of past imperialists are suspect of sharing
the same ambitions and using the same methods. This is
good debating material, but hardly realistic politics. The
lands beyond the Amur, and the present Maritime Province of Siberia were more than a century ago still nominally part of the Manchu empire, not part of the Chinese
state, for no Chinese régime had ever claimed them or
entered them. It is doubtful whether any Han Chinese
prior to Russian annexation had lived or even traded in
these remote and hostile environments. The Manchu
emperors made a clear distinction between their extramural possessions, which were part of their ancestral
kingdom originally established with Mukden (Shenyang)
as its capital, and the Chinese empire of the Ming, which
they acquired in 1644. Chinese (Han) settlement in the
extramural lands was forbidden and the resident Chinese
population of South Manchuria (Liaoning) had been
placed on a different footing from the Chinese subjects
inside the Wall. The Manchurian Chinese, who had been
incorporated into the kingdom before the Ming empire
was conquered, were enrolled, like their Manchu fellow
subjects, in "Banners," the military organization under
which all subjects of the Manchu kingdom had been organized.

It is therefore quite unrealistic to speak of the Maritime Province, the trans-Amur territories, or even the
Ili Valley, as ever having been part of "China." North-
western India, now Pakistan, was a territory of the British Crown, but it was not part of England, and the fate of
the concept of *Algérie Française* is too recent to be for-

gotten. Moreover the situation in the border countries has profoundly altered during the past century. When the Russians annexed the Maritime Province it was estimated that the total inhabitants were some sixteen thousand members of a small tribe distantly connected with the Manchu people. The Russian population of the province now exceeds four million. Beyond the Amur the situation is similar, but the country less inviting to settlers. In Tsarist times there was a considerable Chinese immigrant population who provided the main labor force for the timber industry in the trans-Amur, and had established a thriving commercial colony in Vladivostok. During World War II, on Stalin's orders these immigrants were removed to some unknown destination in the interior of Siberia or Russia, and they never came back. It would seem that insofar as the Chinese have a just cause of complaint regarding these territories, it is rather what Stalin did to their Chinese inhabitants in recent years than what the Tsars' policies were in the mid-nineteenth century. But this does not figure in Chinese polemics.

The Question of War

A war along the Amur, or in the Ili region, is not at all probable. Such a conflict would be even more destructive of the idea of communist unity than other recent events. Neither China nor Russia could hope to gain any commensurate advantage from victory, even if this were possible without a prolonged struggle which would extend far beyond the so-called disputed area. The real beneficiary would be the United States and it is understandable that some writers should look wistfully at the possibility of such a windfall.

On the other hand it is politically difficult for the Chinese, during the open dispute with the USSR, to make this plain to their people. The Army must reflect that Peng Te-huai, once one of their most eminent leaders and an old-time comrade from the Kiangsi Soviet period and the "long march," was disgraced and dismissed for advocating a reconciliation with the USSR and claiming that China needed the Russian alliance and friendship. If Russia is to be convincingly cast in the role of the revisionist power taking the road back to capitalism and imperialism, the suggestion that she still covets further expansion in the northeast and northwest is a more persuasive argument than accusations of collusion with America. Whether in fact the Chinese state and nation gain any advantage from maintaining the quarrel with Russia other than furthering a possible ideological claim to be the true leaders of the communist camp is very doubtful. At the present time this claim is not making much progress and seems unlikely to carry conviction in East Europe. But as it is essential to the whole theory of the Cultural Revolution it is not probable that it will be allowed to lapse.

A Test of Foreign Policy

The recent occupation of Czechoslovakia provided an interesting test of Chinese policy. The USSR, predictably, must be wrong, but the Czechs were just as surely "taking the capitalist road," were clearly being "revisionist" and were therefore equally reprehensible. The Chinese have come out with forthright denunciations of the Russian moves, quite as strongly worded and with more official backing than those uttered in the West. The violation of

the rights of a sovereign state is the gravamen of the
charge. The misguided policies of the Czechs are reproved,
but not, it would seem, held to justify Soviet intervention.
There is logic in this attitude. Russia also accuses Mao
Tse-tung of having destroyed the Chinese Communist
Party, and of following anarchist policies contrary to
the teachings of Marx and Lenin, committing, from an
opposite end of the spectrum, faults as grave as those of
the Czechs. If China accepted the argument that Russia
has the right to restore, by force or threat of force, communist orthodoxy as interpreted in Moscow wherever this
is violated or menaced by innovations, then China herself
could be exposed to such action. Even if that is improbable it would give Russia a status as the leading guardian
of communist purity, which China is at pains to deny.

It may be that there is another calculation at work.
China has, through the excesses of the Cultural Revolution, and in particular during the period in 1967 when
Red Guards dominated and occupied the Ministry of
Foreign Affairs, frightened and annoyed her neighbors,
both Communist and neutralist. It is time to repair this
damage, and by denouncing Russia for violating the sovereignty of Czechoslovakia, China can hope to reassure
Cambodia, Burma, or Nepal—or even North Korea—
that such behavior is wholly outside her conception of
international relations.

China has consistently maintained that the accusation
of "aggression" brought against her is a malicious piece
of imperialist propaganda quite without foundation. If
Korea is cited, she points to the invitation from the sovereign government in Pyongyang, which she recognized,
as full justification for the intervention of the "volunteers."
As the same type of reason is also produced to justify U.S.
and Australian participation in the Vietnamese war, the

Chinese can well think they have rebutted this charge. China claims that Tibet was and has always been an integral part of the Chinese state, and that no foreign power has ever recognized a Tibetan régime *de jure*. Therefore the Chinese decision to enforce their authority in this territory is well within the normal bounds of international law. The Nationalists on Taiwan accept and support this argument, even though they deplore the régime that uses it. As we now see precisely the same argument used to justify the Nigerian reconquest of Biafra—with all the risks that large-scale massacres may be a consequence of their victory—it is difficult to refute the Chinese argument on the legal plane, whatever may be thought of it (or of Biafra) on the moral level. By denouncing Russia for her military action in Czechoslovakia, China therefore wishes to show that she is consistent, and that attempts to tar her with the same brush as Russia are unjust and false.

Peking and the British

These indications of Chinese policy all belong to the period since the eviction of the Red Guards from the Ministry of Foreign Affairs. There seems to be evidence that the extravagances and excesses which were committed in Rangoon, Hong Kong, and elsewhere in 1967 were not part of any Chinese foreign policy, but more probably relate to internal factors. Enthusiasts of the Cultural Revolution took upon themselves the task of propagating its doctrines abroad: ships were painted with Maoist slogans, Chinese schoolchildren in countries outside China were being encouraged to sport Mao badges and paint Mao slogans on

walls. In Hong Kong a minor industrial dispute was
worked up into a strong anti-British agitation, with Maoist inspiration and leadership—or so it was claimed.

The evidence slowly accumulating seems to point to
other interpretations. In Hong Kong the local Communist
organization was well known to be subordinate to headquarters in Canton, and the violent demonstrations, bomb
throwing, and other disorders were inspired by Canton.
At that time the relations between the Canton Party and
Peking were uncertain. Canton was suspected, even accused, of being a stronghold of the "revisionist opposition." Tao Chu, who had risen to fame in the early days
of the Cultural Revolution, had fallen equally fast some
months later, and was now disgraced. But Tao Chu had
been the long-time leader of the Party in Canton. It was
to be supposed that that branch was still a stronghold of
the men he had raised up.

What better way for the Canton cadres to disarm criticism and save themselves from denunciation than to engage in a violent anti-imperialist campaign in Hong
Kong? It proved their revolutionary zeal and could not
be denounced as revisionist. It also annoyed Peking. Peking did not want to open a quarrel with Britain at that
time. Hong Kong is a great earner of foreign exchange
for China, and a valuable port of access and egress. Peking was certainly not ready to try to oust the British, who
must in any case go by the end of the century when the
lease of the New Territories runs out in 1998. Had the
British packed up and gone, who would have come in?
Might it not be the U.S. Seventh Fleet as well as any other
force? Moreover the British were not going quietly, if at
all. They were not in the weak position of the Portuguese
at Macao.

Peking was embarrassed by the Hong Kong agitation.
Unable to avoid giving the agitation verbal support, it

did not want to see a serious crisis develop. The confidence with which the Hong Kong government assumed that this was the real situation is remarkable. It almost suggests some very reliable information. But the Red Guards in Peking could not understand these political subtleties. They violently demonstrated against the British and burned down the British Embassy Chancery. The police did not restrain them, because the police do not know where they stand today. Although no apology has been made, there have been hints that it was not approved in high circles. It was a very delicate time for the leaders, such as Chou En-lai, who had not been attacked, but yet were from time to time trying to set bounds to Red Guard excess. The Hong Kong agitation died away, and the troubles of Canton itself, which has been a center of the most acute factional brawling between Red Guard groups, preoccupied the local leadership. Very gradually the Chinese seem to be groping for a relaxation of tension with Britain. Exit permits for diplomats due to return home, denied for a year and more, are now granted.

The Diplomats

The wild and far from diplomatic conduct of the staff of the Chinese Embassy in London at this time may well be due to other causes, and apply equally to similar behavior elsewhere. Chinese diplomats abroad were placed in a very difficult situation by the Cultural Revolution. They learned that at home people like themselves were under attack, denunciation, and sometimes physical assault. Even to ride in an official car had provoked Red Guard rage and violence. In foreign, above all Western, capitals, the Chinese staff, although having few contacts

among their colleagues or the general population, still
certainly lived like diplomats. They dressed in foreign
clothes, rode in cars, dwelt in good houses. They mixed
to some extent with "bourgeois" people, even if only in
the course of duty. All this was highly dangerous. At
any moment some zealous employee might (and some
did) denounce his ambassador as a revisionist, a bourgeois, a secret supporter of Liu Shao-chi. It became essential to make some clear and public demonstration of
the purity of their Maoist thinking, and the most obvious
way to get this message across, by means of the world
press, was a brawl with the London police, the representatives of the bourgeois imperialist régime. A few
broken heads and bruised limbs were a small price to
pay for demonstrating true revolutionary zeal and complete adherence to the Cultural Revolution.

During this period, when the Red Guards and their
supporters controlled the premises of the Ministry of
Foreign Affairs, unauthorized telegrams were allegedly
sent to Chinese missions abroad. It is not clear what instructions they contained, but it would seem probable
that they did not discourage vehement pro-Maoist demonstrations. It is not hard to see what a situation this
created for the overseas staff: they could not tell who
was in control in Peking, nor for how long they would
remain in ignorance. If they ignored instructions coming
from the Ministry they would be victimized were the control to remain in Red Guard hands, and probably receive
no thanks or recognition from the normal administration
if it recovered authority. It was clearly wise to obey
instructions, no matter who might have sent them, so long
as they came from the Ministry.

The outbreak of these demonstrations among overseas
embassy staff and their cessation when order was restored
in the Ministry seems to suggest very strongly that they

were due to the fears of the personnel abroad and their anxiety to cover themselves against any eventuality. It is worth observing also that almost all ambassadors (except the one in Cairo) had been recalled to Peking and that the London Embassy was in charge of the cultural counselor during the period of violence. Violence and excesses have been reproved, and more recently condemned, by the leaders of the régime, but these reproofs have always been in general terms. Specific instances are not held up as bad examples. The forces of moderation have not hitherto felt strong enough to back their disapproval by citing cases and proceeding to punishment.

Nor has repentance gone very far. Neither Britain nor India has received any apology. Burma, where Maoist Chinese schoolboys demonstrating and flaunting Mao badges provoked a counterattack by Burmese mobs, in which the Chinese and their resident community suffered loss and damage, is still harshly abused by the Chinese radio, and relations between the two countries, formerly unusually good, have touched a very low point. Nepal has been cold-shouldered, and only Cambodia, where Prince Sihanouk reacted strongly to early Maoist activities, has received soothing words from Chou En-lai and promises of continued friendship. This may be significant, since Cambodia, in relation to the war in Vietnam, occupies a position of much greater direct importance than any of the other countries subjected to provocative assaults.

Damage Done

Even if it were now clear that moderation will prevail, there can be no doubt that this series of episodes has done China much harm. Men like Chou En-lai and Chen Yi, the foreign minister (himself under criticism for some time), are far too experienced in international relations not to know what foreign reactions have been, and that in Asia in particular much of the diplomatic gains of the past fifteen years has been dissipated. China had, even among nations not at all sympathetic to her régime and philosophy, gained respect as a scrupulous upholder of normal diplomatic immunities and courtesies. The burning of embassies in such places as Jakarta was, it was hinted, what might be expected of "fascist" régimes, but was quite beyond the range of possibility where Communist discipline prevailed. This reputation is now lost.

Nor can it be said, with any conviction, that if China was prepared to sacrifice these advantages when dealing with non-Communist powers, her policy has in other respects made compensating gains. Insofar as any distinctive foreign policy can be associated with the Cultural Revolution it would appear to be revolutionary extremism. The Cultural Revolution has been hailed as the first wave of the new revolutionary flood, which it is claimed will make the Russian October Revolution and the first Chinese Communist revolution appear by contrast almost insignificant.

These effects are not yet perceived outside Peking. In West Europe and elsewhere some of the student movements have been to a degree influenced by Mao and his thoughts, but it would often appear that Mao is quoted and his name chanted more as a badge of rebellion and opposition to the establishment than as an example to be followed. The virtual dismantling of the Chinese Communist Party has been seen with dismay among the Communists of Europe and Asia. As a program for world revolution the Cultural Revolution is almost wholly negative. It has propounded no new method of removing from power the established forces hostile to communism, and it has weakened and confused the existing Communist parties and their sympathizers. It would almost appear possible that the loud reiteration of these goals by the leaders of the Cultural Revolution masks an inward realization that in fact foreign policy has been sacrificed to the emotional demands of the internal struggle.

Demonstrations and disorders at home and abroad are not a policy—rather they represent a breakdown of control. Hostility to Russia and to America are inheritances from the previous period which, being in themselves harmonious enough with the working of the Cultural Revolution, need not be changed. The development of the nuclear weapons program, more a matter of national defense than of foreign policy, has, like the Army itself, been kept as much as possible out of the battle. The Army may have been to some degree drawn into the struggle, but the fact that the Cultural Revolution has not, as far as can be known, frustrated or even seriously hindered the development of the nuclear program suggests that somewhere, at some point, limits were set and have been obeyed. Chou En-lai, as long ago as 1966, was reported as saying that the Cultural Revolution and Red Guard activity could not be extended to Sinkiang since this was an area of vital national importance. He never needed to say this twice, and it does not seem to have produced any critical response.

China Can Wait

Responsible and able leaders may sincerely believe that if a great political movement, designed to renew the moral fiber of the nation, can guard the régime and the revolution against decadence and inspire the people to new

achievements that will bring these great goals within
reach, certain sacrifices must be accepted. China has in
the past lived to herself. It may be necessary for her to do
so again until the great transformation of society is perfected. Her new strength will then make possible a foreign
policy whose goals are more easily attainable than those
of past efforts. Lost ground will be made up very rapidly
when backed with overwhelming strength. In the meantime certain activities, such as nuclear power, which directly foster that coming strength and can back those
future policies must be preserved from thoughtless or
overenthusiastic interference.

The Chinese may have decided that with their present
resources and in the present configuration of world power
their aims cannot be achieved without unacceptable risk.
America will not be ejected from the continent of Asia,
still less from its adjoining islands and seas, by slogans or
by limited local revolutionary activity.

Russia will not lose her pre-eminence in the Communist
world movement by the mere fact of Chinese criticism
and opposition. But time will alter these conditions. The
American people may tire of endless commitments to up-
hold in Asia régimes which are unable to muster popular
support. Soviet domination in East Europe is of a character
to rouse more opposition than loyalty. The time may come
when China, as the Chinese will believe, renewed and
infinitely more powerful, will be the incontestable leader
of the revolutionary forces of the world. It is dogma that
these forces must ultimately triumph, and Russia has, in
Chinese eyes, forfeited her right to the leadership by following revisionist roads. The first task is therefore to carry
through in China itself that great operation of national
and social reconstruction which will ensure that Chinese
society is never exposed to the dangers to which they believe the Russians have succumbed. This will take time,

perhaps years. Meanwhile material strength can be built up.

Foreign policy, unable at present to achieve its aims and faced, as in the past few years, with numerous failures, due primarily to the weakness of the force behind it, must be laid aside or continued only in a minor key. Chou En-lai once answered a foreign journalist who had inquired whether China was not anxious to regain her seat in the United Nations with the words: "China can wait." There is also a proverb, "Let the water flow and the stones will appear."

The assumption supporting this expectation is that the Cultural Revolution will prove to have accomplished the aims which Mao Tse-tung was seeking, and that therefore the virtual renunciation of any constructive foreign policy for some years to come is a worthwhile sacrifice of the national interest. But this assumption is by no means verified yet, and may never be. In the complex and confusing scene which China now presents there are at least as many indications that the Cultural Revolution is failing to attain its goals as there are portents of success. Many foreign observers have now assumed that in reality the whole movement is grinding to a halt, and the growing need to use military officers to preside over governmental organs proves that the movement set itself an impossible task. It may be expected that there will be no formal repudiation of Mao or his "thought"—that while he lives his ideas will remain official symbols. Thereafter they may be increasingly ignored by men who have practical problems to face and solve. This view of the outcome is widely held abroad. How far it is shared by silent doubters in China cannot be known.

A New Foreign Policy

Should it prove to be a correct, or a near guess, it must greatly alter the Chinese approach to foreign policy. If the dream of coming world revolutionary movements headed by China is quietly put aside as Utopian, it will be necessary to take a cool look at the actual position of China and her past and recent policies. These have been marked by the dual hostility toward the United States and the USSR—the two most powerful nations in the world, the nations which respectively control the Pacific Ocean and the northern lands neighboring China, the sea power and the land power, the only two who can ever directly threaten or invade the Chinese homelands. This very dangerous situation can only be justified by the belief that before long one or the other, or both the opponents, will be disrupted by internal disorders and become inactive as threats. Leaders who would have discarded, albeit privately, the expectations of the Cultural Revolution will not hold this belief. They must seek a new policy which will divide rather than unite their opponents.

There is no valid third choice. None of the other world powers, in Asia or in Europe, can provide an adequate counterpoise to the power of the United States in the east and south or to the power of the Soviet Union in the north. Nor is there any chance that China could construct a new block of such powers. Sooner or later China must seek détente either with the U.S., in order to face Russia, or with Russia to oppose the U.S. The second alternative is much the more likely choice. The quarrel with Russia remains mainly theoretical: the two nations have no real grievance against each other. Russia does not seek to annex any Chinese territory, and the view that China hopes to recover lost Manchu lands in the north is not realistic.

If a change in leadership in Russia or in China, perhaps nearly coinciding in both countries, were to occur it would not be too difficult to put forward the view that "revisionism" had been checked by the inherent communist virtue of the Russian people, who could once more be welcomed as comrades in the great struggle against imperialism. If relations between Russia and America worsen as a result of the Czech crisis and a tougher policy by a new administration in America, this development could come quite soon.

On the other hand, the prospects for détente with the United States do not seem promising. The war in Vietnam continues. There is no certainty that it will soon be brought to an end or, if it is, that the settlement achieved would be satisfactory in Chinese eyes. The administration of President Nixon seems unlikely to make radical changes in U.S. policy which China could accept. Whereas no fundamental issues divide China and Russia, gulfs remain between any variety of Chinese foreign policy and those of the United States. China will not rest until her influence is paramount in Southeast Asia, but the United States is not ready to renounce any part in the future of Eastern Asia. Chinese leaders will have little difficulty in deciding that Russia is the more favorable option. Mao's own thoughts—and words—when he is no longer there to place a new interpretation upon them, can be cited to support such a change. "We lean to one side," he said shortly after his régime came to power in China. The side was that of the Soviet.

Some Sung philosophers compared the untrained nature of man at birth to "water whirling in a gorge" which would take whatever outlet was most accessible, whether good or bad. Chinese foreign policy is now whirling aimlessly in the gorge of the Cultural Revolution; we cannot see which outlet it will take, but before long it must find its future course, either good or bad.

One-Man Diplomacy?

Richard Harris

No one could disagree with Professor Fitzgerald's view that the Cultural Revolution has brought about a hiatus in Chinese foreign policy, thereby giving students of China an opportunity to check on past errors and examine the conventional wisdom. Of course the revelations of the last two years have thrown much more light on the inner workings of the Chinese Communist Party than they have on the formation of its external attitudes. These attitudes, as expressed in action during the Cultural Revolution, have simply kept their old momentum. An *ad hoc* response to events, where necessary, best describes Peking's action.

To put Fitzgerald's careful analysis into a wider context, however, I should like to begin with the question: Can a country that pursues a foreign policy possibly bring about a hiatus in it? To talk about this hiatus we must first dismiss from our minds those concepts of "foreign policy" as a product of the Western system of nation states formulated over the last three centuries. We must analyze China's international behavior without the distortion of those Western concepts.

To do so, one must begin by separating China's attitude to the world beyond her borders from her clear na-

tional objectives of regaining control over territories lost
to her during the era of "unequal" treaties. Included are
those border settlements similarly arrived at. It is necessary to make this distinction because far too many people
still rest their case on China as an expansionist power, because of her invasion of Tibet in 1950. Yet no student
of China can be in any doubt that all Chinese believed
that Tibet was part of the China that had been despoiled
or dismembered in the age of imperialism, and that, consequently, China was in no sense crossing an international
frontier by subduing Tibet.

There were other Chinese claims: Mongolia, which
had to be abandoned by treaty in the face of Russian
power, and Hong Kong and Macao, set aside for later
settlement. This leaves Taiwan, itself the most emotion-
ally charged because of its loss to Japan in 1895, and still
the one issue which, if modified by a shift of American
policy, would more than any other affect China's attitude toward the world. All through the years, even when
China's attitude toward the outside world was expressed in
the most fulsomely revolutionary language, there remained
this awkward but inescapable national claim to justice. It
came out once again in the communiqué following the
October 13-31 meeting of the Central Committee in Peking last year; tucked in among all the ideological jargon
was the blunt statement: We are determined to liberate
Taiwan.

It cannot be overemphasized that Taiwan lies at the
root of China's hatred of the United States. President
Truman's action in 1950, resulting in the support of the
rival government of Chiang Kai-shek, exposed the one
major unfulfilled task of the Chinese revolution—the
restoration of China's unity.

Here Professor Fitzgerald deals suitably with the territories across the Amur in eastern Siberia: it is a splendid

issue to bring up when the Chinese want to taunt the Russians, and the Chinese sense of righteousness is inflated thereby. But it is not an active territorial claim. Nor, for the most part, are borders "unequally" settled elsewhere the subject of actual territorial claims. Resentment and some emotional recompense are what seem to be in the minds of China's leaders. Only in the case of India, because the border touched on a rebellious Tibet, was China caught unprepared. The reaction was the sharper because at that time Mao Tse-tung's view of a revolutionary world was beginning to obliterate the policy of coexistence that China had earlier initiated.

China and the Outside World

In turning to the evidence of China's behavior toward the outside world I begin therefore by dismissing the concept of foreign policy. Before the war it was a common Western view of China's plight in the face of Japanese aggression that she must improve her relations with the Soviet Union since she could not face enemies on both her eastern and northern flanks. How much more is this true today with China facing the United States on the east and the Soviet Union to the north. Yet when both were being treated as enemies China proceeded willfully to add India on another flank. Can this be the action of a country considering foreign policy in a Western sense?

"Yes" might be the answer if we recognize that China is a revolutionary power, bent on taking up from the Russians the leadership of a world revolutionary force. Insofar as this is true—and it plainly has become more and more true since about 1958—it is the work of one man, Mao Tse-tung. To make sense of China's international behavior both during the Cultural Revolution and in the past, I find it easier to separate Mao's personality and ambitions from the rest of the Chinese leadership.

Insofar as an alternative to Mao's policy evolved, and could well have gone on evolving until China had something like a foreign policy, it did so after the shock of the Korean war had fallen on an unprepared and initially uninvolved China. The policy that emerged after the Korean armistice was one of coexistence, especially with Asian neutralist neighbors—few African states were at that time independent—but including European capitalist powers which had recognized the new China. It is instructive to recall that as late as 1956 *People's Daily* could welcome the progress being made by the British government on the path of coexistence.

This coexistence policy quickly adjusted itself to the imperative that if good relations with potentially friendly (because neutralist-inclined) Asian neighbors were to be promoted, then it followed that the overseas Chinese could not be treated other than as citizens of the country, nor could any Communist or revolutionary movement opposed to the government with which China had established diplomatic relations be supported. In either case such elements in the population had to take second place in the calculation of China's interests.

It was after 1958 that this policy began slowly to be overlaid by the revolutionary attitude of Mao Tse-tung. Mao may well have held this view all along, allowing the coexistence pressed by Chou En-lai, and culminating at Bandung in 1955, to be pushed against his better judgment. We know that in these early years Mao's role in policy making was limited. But since 1958 Mao has been seriously concerned with what he regards as revisionism in Russia. In consequence, China's policy of coexistence has been eroded. The emphasis on revolution has steadily

displaced it to the point that at the height of the Cultural Revolution even countries like Burma have been
rejected in favor of declared Chinese support for a Communist revolutionary opposition movement.

Mao and His Colleagues

It is the almost exclusive concern of Mao Tse-tung with
these developments that dominates current events. Lin
Piao may be included with Mao, of course, but one cannot
say with certainty that any other Chinese leader is wholly
identified with this view. Whatever mutual understanding
or shrewd judgment of personal interests has brought
Chou En-lai over to Mao's side in any conflict within the
Chinese Communist Party, we may be sure that the views
he pressed at Bandung or the influence he brought to bear
over Vietnam at Geneva in 1954 are his real views, which
he has had to abandon or suppress during the course of
the Cultural Revolution. That he was able to step in after
the rebels took over the Chinese Foreign Office in August
1967 only shows that he has tried to restrain the worst
excesses. Since then there has been no new initiative in
foreign affairs coming from Chou, nor does it seem likely
that there will be when so much confusion and damage
remain to be cleared up internally.

What is true of Chou is true in varying degrees of all
Mao's other—now disgraced—colleagues. We need hardly
doubt that the development of the Sino-Soviet dispute
found Mao with plenty of backers. Had not some Chinese
leaders—including Peng Chen—been criticized earlier
for their premature anti-Russian attitudes? Is there not a
basic contempt for the Russians which most Chinese could
have shared, especially at the thought of subservience to

Stalin while he lived, knowing of his role in the past and his insistence on Russian economic and strategic interests in the 1950 agreements?

But if one looks at this broadly nationalist attitude alongside of the events of the Sino-Soviet dispute and Mao's part in them, is it possible to see it as a collective policy reached by the government in Peking, or must it not be a struggle conducted by Mao personally for ends that are often personal to him as a revolutionary leader, however much he could imagine them to be in China's interests as a revolutionary power?

I would suggest that there is no reason to look upon the developments of the 1960s—the "support" of revolutionary movements, the attempts to encourage pro-Maoist splinter parties in the Communist movement, or the wanton changing of friends into enemies—as in any way a phenomenon of Chinese foreign policy, but simply as an exposition of Mao's own ambitions and his conviction of his righteousness as a revolutionary. One is almost tempted to suggest that Liu Shao-chi's probable advocacy of continued good relations with General Ne Win of Burma—he had more than once visited the country— was enough for Mao to reverse the policy followed there. And the longer this phase has gone on the more wildly inaccurate is China's view of the world situation.

This is not to say that the original policy of coexistence has even now been totally obliterated. Nepal and Afghanistan and some African countries are still on tolerable terms with Peking. Other countries like Pakistan, whose position in relation to two of China's (i.e., Mao's) enemies (India and Russia) is crucial, may be cultivated under what seems the old pretext of coexistence, but for the most part the momentum of today is the momentum Mao has given to Chinese attitudes.

Mao's Foreign Policy

These attitudes are so personal that it is difficult to make any judgment about "Chinese" foreign policy while Mao is still in control. He is plainly directing affairs in China, even if, in the sphere of foreign policy, he does no more than inhibit others. Since the words used in Peking are as intransigent and the view of the world as narrow as ever, it is Mao's policy we have to worry about. Is this or is this not the serious threat that John Foster Dulles and Dean Rusk feared almost equally? The answer is almost certainly no, and a great part of the reason, as Fitzgerald has pointed out, comes from Mao's own cautiousness. Despite the extremism and hysteria of the Cultural Revolution that has given China such a bad image and huddled almost the whole diplomatic corps in Peking into one solid group regardless of their antagonistic governments, it is Chairman Mao who, strangely enough, can be relied on to keep the peace. However far he is driven by his personal obsessions in "struggling" with the Russians, or "supporting" revolutionary movements—as a theorist of the people's war, as a strategist for the overthrow of imperialism, or as an inflated messiah collecting disciples—in all this Mao is no adventurer. Those who fear Mao's success need only look at the results of his revolutionary policy over the past four or five years to conclude that however shrewd a tactician Mao has proved to be on his own ground, he is inherently incapable of becoming the focus of a new world revolutionary force.

Two Documents

These fears of China were principally stimulated by two documents. The first was a speech made by the now over-thrown "pro-capitalist" Liu Shao-chi in December 1949, when he recommended the Chinese revolution as a model for Asia to follow. In the West, and in the United States especially, this was immediately taken to mean that China was going to impose its revolution on Southeast Asia and such other parts of the continent as Chinese power might penetrate. Chinese participation in the Korean war a year later was taken as proof of expansionist intentions, and thereafter, despite lack of evidence, these intentions have been accepted without question by almost all strategic thinkers in the West.

The second document was Lin Piao's analysis of people's war in September 1965, once again read as a statement of Chinese intentions. Even now this attitude lives on in official American thinking, although half a dozen American scholars have analyzed Lin's words, and though there are differences of emphasis among them, all agree that action by China is the one thing that is not promised by Lin's doctrine.

The Principle of Acknowledgment

If we look at Mao's behavior toward the forces of world revolution, can we not see at work a principle surviving from China's past? Mao is not much of a traveler: two visits to Moscow—the first unavoidable, the second a desperate attempt to turn the tide of revisionism—are all the traveling he has done in a lifetime, though he could easily have been received in state in a dozen Asian or African capitals in the last ten years or so. But emperors in the old China did not go on trips either. Tribute missions came to them and knocked their heads on the ground thrice as a mark of submission. Of course Mao does not consciously see himself in a similar role, but might not the same principle be at work? It is the principle of acknowledgment. In the last six hundred years China has not been outgoing or expansionist (Cheng Ho's voyages in the early Ming are the exception), but rather indrawing and static. China's status was acknowledged by those who came to a great and civilized country.

Has there not been the same undertone in Mao's cultivation of visiting revolutionaries from Africa or Latin America or Asia? Is there not, in the patronage now offered to the Communist guerrillas of Thailand or Burma or Malaysia the same patronage that was given to Southeast Asia in China's past? Is not the same acknowledgment of the supremacy of the "thoughts" of Mao as the only sure guide to revolution required of them before this patronage is conferred? It has not been the Chinese on missions away from China who have made China's power and glory but outside missions going to China that have come to acknowledge it.

But now we see that the tributaries have grown fewer and fewer. At the October 1968 ceremony Albania was the only Communist government, New Zealand's the leading Communist party, to be represented. At most Mao can console himself with the thought that among the younger generation in the West, turning away from conventional communism, there are some who have found in him something of a leader if a poor second as a revolutionary to the much more romantic figure of Che Guevara.

We cannot, I would suggest, take Mao's support of revolutionary movements seriously, in the sense of possibly bringing into power movements that might not have won power except for Chinese aid. Nor does it look as though any of the guerrilla movements supported by China in Thailand or the Malaysia border or Burma have any hope of success. In Africa and Latin America hardly any active following is left to Chinese patronage. That the search for those ready to acknowledge Maoism will continue while Mao lasts we need not doubt. A man who has carried his own struggle within China as far as Mao has— forecasting the need for three or four cultural revolutions every century—is not going to be put off by his apparent failure to win a world following for his revolutionary leadership.

"Some comrades will ask," said a senior official of the Maoist camp last July, addressing a meeting of cadres in Peking, "in what respect can the present situation be described as excellent? Since China is opposed everywhere and setbacks are encountered everywhere, how can the situation be described as good?" To which his answer, whether or not it satisfied his audience, was: "What is most important is the existence of China, the existence of socialist China that clings to Mao Tse-tung's thought . . . in the greatest turmoil there is China to hold the fort." Thus does socialism in one country take a new form.

Looking back over nearly twenty years of Communist China then, we may distinguish the emergence of a policy of coexistence, cautiously pursued toward those of China's neighbors who were neutralist, even hopeful about capitalist Western Europe. But if this was a foreign policy, shaping itself on a rational understanding of the facts of the world and of China's situation, it was soon scotched by the stronger pressures that Mao Tse-tung brought to China's relations with the world.

So where does this leave us? If Chinese thinking about foreign policy hardly coincides with our own, Chinese fears of outside attack are very active indeed. There was undoubtedly a fierce debate in China in 1965 over the likelihood of Chinese involvement in the Vietnam war. This had its influence as the Cultural Revolution was taking shape. But some time in 1966, when it seems probable that assurances were exchanged in the Sino-American talks in Warsaw, China's fears were lessened, and Mao's policy of non-involvement, advising the Vietnamese on how they should react to vast numbers of Americans (advice that the Vietnamese ignored), could stand. Thereafter, as Fitzgerald suggests, the Cultural Revolution has largely ignored foreign issues, though of late anxieties about a Russian attack have been fomented by major Russian reinforcement of its eastern frontier, coupled with Chinese assumptions about a convergence of attitude between Russia and America.

America has now got over the old fears of a global communist conspiracy in which Russia, China, North Korea, and North Vietnam were all close and unshakable partners. Now the triangle of big powers splits up differently. The USSR fear is an American rapprochement with China —but that fear should be modified once a settlement in Vietnam opens the door wider to a détente between America and Russia. The Chinese fear is of a ganging up —already virtually a reality according to their propaganda—between Russia and America. Here a détente between these two would only tend to confirm China's fears. So we are left with what hope there is either for change within China or change from the United States.

Change Under Mao?

I cannot share Professor Fitzgerald's hope of real change in China while Mao is still actively in command of the Cultural Revolution. Chou En-lai may have been able to restore the status quo at the Chinese Foreign Office after its takeover by "rebels" in August 1967; he has not been able or has not dared to do more. There are no signs at all of China "groping" for a relaxation of tension with Britain or with any other Western European power. The granting of exit permits to diplomats is no more than the barest return to diplomatic decencies.

No, it seems that the same pressures that make the Cultural Revolution concentrate on internal struggles, or now on reorganization and stabilization, also inhibit any action by a potentially rational man such as Chou En-lai, who might try to restore to external affairs some of the old coexistence policy. And is it not probable that Mao has no positive desire for friendly relations with anyone? The man who saw in 1945 "the irresistible force of the Chinese people, . . . a force that will burst forth and supplant both foreign oppression and feudal oppression" had no vision of a China surrounded by peaceful and friendly neighbors. And he will never turn his mind to such a possibility until China's unity and independence, which formed his vision in 1945, attain their fulfillment.

So we are back to Taiwan. There will be no real change in China until there is change in an American policy which recognizes and upholds militarily, economically, and politically a rival government of China. That is something no Chinese can stomach and it is the reason why the United States will remain the enemy of the new China.

The present year looks to be a time of consolidation in China. The Maoist revolutionary committees are nominally in control throughout the country. The character of these committees, in which the Army is almost everywhere the dominant force, makes it very difficult to tell whether China will be ruled strongly from the center, or whether —as the long-heralded Ninth Party Congress may soon reveal to us—the remodeled Communist Party will again be able to recapture the prestige of the old one whose leadership Mao Tse-tung destroyed in his Cultural Revolution. That means that it is difficult even to foretell a return to China's awareness of the outside world, much less a readiness to see a world of nation-states instead of a world of revolutionaries and counterrevolutionaries.

"China has in the past lived to herself," writes Professor Fitzgerald. But he also suggests—and I would agree with him—that however much Mao may superficially have triumphed over his internal enemies, he has not and cannot achieve the objectives of the Cultural Revolution. It therefore follows that China must one day turn away from her dream of world revolution. It is hard to imagine a man as obsessed as Mao, now past his seventy-fifth birthday, being capable of this change. But it might not be out of the question that an aging Mao, able to proclaim his victory, might once again retreat to the "second line," to be succeeded as a policy maker by others. There must soon emerge from the turmoil of the Cultural Revolution some of the forces of order and progress which will be ready to pay lip service to Maoism but will begin to take China back, in foreign policy, to the coexistence and rationality current during the productive fifties.

I would differ from Professor Fitzgerald only in being more skeptical about the degree of hostility to the USSR, as a matter of policy. This seems much more a product of

Mao Tse-tung's personal struggles than a considered Chinese hostility. Was the partnership between China and the Soviet Union ever really ideological? I question whether there is any evidence of close cooperation between the Communist parties of the two nations from 1949 to 1956, when the dispute began. For Mao, yes: his relationship to Stalin was a vital link. But for China as a whole was it not the aid and the alliance that mattered and very little else? In other words, that after Mao's personal vendetta can be buried or tamed, China can quite easily resume equable state relations with the USSR without bothering about the exact nature of the creed to which they are both nominally attached. This might have the beneficial effect of hurrying the change in the USSR itself. She will no longer need to pretend to be the leader of a world movement whose separate members are all now chafing at the restraints imposed upon them.

This still leaves an area of Western overanxiety extending back twenty years—Southeast Asia. Here again I remain skeptical about a "Chinese" as distinct from a Maoist revolutionary policy. Professor Fitzgerald thinks that China will not rest until her influence is paramount in Southeast Asia. I would reverse the statement and say that China will remain disturbed so long as American power is present there in force. China's relations with the states of Southeast Asia did seem in the days of coexistence to be falling back into a pattern very like the old: the paternal, aid-giving China patting on the head the good, neutralist children who were unwilling to ally themselves with China's enemy. But Chinese influence? It seems to me this takes us into a sphere of Chinese foreign policy not yet matured in the minds of China's present generation of leaders. It may well become matured in the next. But of that generation we could hardly know less than we do.

An Isolationist Science Policy

John M. H. Lindbeck

For almost a decade China has been going her own rather lonely way. Fear of dependence on others seems to have deep roots in China. About a hundred years ago one of China's early modernizers and notable military and vice-regal figures, Tso Tsung-tang, phrased the Chinese position even more sharply than Mao: "The method of self-strengthening should be to seek from among ourselves, not seek from among others. He who seeks the help of others will be controlled by others, and he who relies upon himself will have the situation under his control."

In the brief century of officially approved Chinese importation of modern scientific, technological, and educational resources from abroad, the priorities—if it is possible to differentiate between inherently related and intermixed elements of the broad revolution wrought by modern science—have remained the same. First of all China wanted modern military technology, then science, and finally education. Beginning in the 1860s, it was officially recognized that internal authority and external power depended on modern weapons. The suppression of the Taiping rebels underlined the melancholy utility of and the Chinese belief in such technologies for domestic power, which was finally summed up by Mao Tse-tung in the chill phrase that "political power grows out of the barrel of a gun." In the world arena, the humiliation of foreign intrusions and repeated military defeats at the hands of Western powers and Japan led to the establishment of the Kiangnan Arsenal at Shanghai in 1865 and then to the detonation of a nuclear device in 1964. The technologies and basic production facilities for these achievements were imported. Studies in specialized centers to develop a small scientific and engineering elite were developed later, but prior to 1960 China basically still depended on foreign institutions to produce the small talented corps of scientists and engineers she needed for her most urgent military and technological purposes.

The first experiment in training Chinese abroad took one hundred and twenty Chinese students to the United States in 1872 and thirty students to England and France in 1876. This program was terminated abruptly in 1881 with nothing to replace it.

By 1905, when an imperial decree abolished the traditional examination system, the institutional and traditional barriers to educational modernization as a national process were breached. However, despite the efforts of private agencies from the West, mostly missionary in auspices, and the Chinese national and local authorities, very little progress was achieved in the first half of the twentieth century because of political instability, international intrusions, and revolutionary chaos. There was a brief period of forward motion after the Chinese Nationalist Party came to power in 1928—with the establishment of science academies, research laboratories, new and expanded school systems, and the development of institutional channels that were intended to bring China systematically into the mainstreams of world science, technology, and education. But this modest start—restricted by domestic military conflicts with the Communist Party, which proposed alternate strategies for modernization and reflected the ambitions of rival social groups—was effectively terminated with the Japanese invasion of China in 1937. Not until the Communists came to power in 1949 was there again opportunity for developing systematic large-scale programs for advancing science, technology, and modern education in China.

Since the launching of the Great Proletarian Cultural Revolution in 1966, promising openings to the world community of modern science and technology have again been blocked by China's domestic preoccupations, her ambivalence about her role in the international system, and the Maoist ideological mold that places severe constraints on giving first place to producing an environment conducive to rapid scientific growth despite Mao's own desire to enhance China's modern military, technological, and scientific capabilities.

Prior to 1966, however, Communist China was strongly committed to the spread of modern scientific ideas and technical skills. Because they were able to unify the Chinese Mainland and to establish effective political and social controls over the country, China's new leaders were in a position to hasten the process of change. They quickly worked out plans to systematize the way in which the scientific outlook and modern industrial and related technologies could be spread rapidly throughout the country. The Chinese embarked on the greatest educational experiment in history, one designed to convert China in the brief span of one generation from a country of illiterate peasants into a society with a literate population informed by the essential principles of modern science and the practical technological skills that are associated with these. Considering its initial level of retardation, the Chinese accomplishment over the past decade and a half is thus far unprecedented and, if sustained, could place China within ten to twenty years among the leading contributors to world science and technology. China now has about two million people who have had some form of higher education whereas in 1949 there were only about 125,000 college graduates. Of the two million, about 125,000 are trained in the natural sciences and over 600,000 in various branches of engineering. Few of these are holders of advanced higher degrees, and many, if not most, have not had the equivalent of the first higher degree as recognized abroad. However, they have had some advanced specialized training.

For achieving major scientific, technological, and educational progress, the groups of critical importance are those with sufficient training to provide direction to the work of the less well trained.

Before 1950, China had turned primarily to Europe, the United States, and Japan for modern science and technology. Her debt to these countries for training the first generation of scientists is documented in the table, shown on page 186, which was taken from Cheng Chuyuan, "Scientific and Engineering Manpower in Communist China," in U.S. Congress, Joint Economic Committee, *An Economic Profile of Mainland China* (Washington, D.C.: U.S. Government Printing Office, 1967), Vol. 2, p. 542. These scholars, scientists, and engineers trained in Japan and the West have provided the Communist régime with its basic pool of talent for building and energizing its own educational, scientific, and industrial establishments. But Peking chose to break this pattern of scholarly and scientific communications with the West. However, Chinese needs in 1950 were vast and the new leaders of China set out to speed the introduction and development of resources necessary to modernize the nation. To meet these needs, a Russian orientation replaced the earlier relations with the West. The Japanese connections had been severed earlier by the war that began in 1937.

Chinese interactions with the external world since 1950 have gone through several stages: massive borrowing from the Soviet Union, 1950-60; the break with the USSR followed by limited and exploratory policies of finding non-Communist substitute sources for Russian scientific and technical assistance, 1960-66; and following the launching of the Cultural Revolution, the breakdown of scholarly and scientific communications with the rest of the world, 1966 to date.

During the decade of Sino-Soviet cooperation a massive transfer of information, skill, and technology took place. Some 11,000 Soviet specialists were sent to China, a large percentage of whom assisted in helping to construct and place in operation the one hundred and thirty major industrial projects that Russia undertook to construct for the Chinese. Over seven hundred Russian scientists helped the Chinese develop a new educational system. Between 1950 and 1956, about fifty Russian scientists came to help establish programs and institutes of scientific research; this number jumped to about eight hundred between 1957 and 1960. Public administration absorbed seven hundred and fifty Russian advisers and about 3,700 assisted the Chinese in such fields as communication and transportation, agriculture, water conservation, forestry, and public health. (C. Y. Cheng, *Scientific and Engineering Manpower in Communist China, 1949-1963*, National Science Foundation, Washington, D.C.: U.S. Government Printing Office.)

Lacking adequate facilities in China, about 38,000 Chinese benefited from Russia's educational and training resources at all levels, as indicated in the table shown on page 191, which was taken from Cheng Chu-

Estimated Number of Western and Japanese Trained Degree-Holders in Science, Medicine, and Engineering, 1850-1962

PLACE	YEAR	NUMBER AWARDED DEGREES, ALL FIELDS[1]	NUMBER AWARDED DOCTORAL DEGREES, ALL FIELDS[1]	NUMBER AWARDED DEGREES IN SCIENCES, ENGINEERING, OR MEDICINE[1]	HOLDERS OF DEGREES IN SCIENCES, ENGINEERING, OR MEDICINE AND STAYING IN COMMUNIST CHINA[2]	SCIENTISTS, ENGINEERS, AND MEDICAL DOCTORS HOLDING PH.D. DEGREES AND STAYING IN COMMUNIST CHINA[2]
United States and Canada	1850-1953	13,800	2,100	6,000	2,000	450
Japan	1901-39	12,000	100	4,500	1,500	50
Great Britain	1911-49	2,500	346	1,000	500	120
France	1907-62	3,000	582	1,200	500	150
Germany	1907-62	3,500	731	2,000	800	250
Other West European countries	1907-62	1,500	258	800	200	80
TOTAL		36,300	4,117	15,500	5,500	1,100

[1] Includes those on the Chinese Mainland and those staying abroad.
[2] Does not take into account losses during the period as the result of death or retirement. The number of those actually working in Communist China in 1962 may have been 15 to 20 percent less than shown.

yuan, "Scientific and Engineering Manpower in Communist China," in U.S. Congress, Joint Economic Committee, *An Economic Profile of Mainland China* (Washington, D.C.: U.S. Government Printing Office, 1967), Vol. 2, p. 541.

In addition, under a 1954 agreement with Russia, the Chinese received on exchange large amounts of scientific and technical data. By 1960, this included over 10,000 sets of blueprints and design specifications covering a wide variety of machinery and plant construction, over 240,000 books and journals for the Peking National Library, and a large amount of laboratory and research equipment. Lesser amounts of aid, but by no means insignificant, came from the Communist countries of East Europe to which the Chinese also sent students (about five hundred to seven hundred for specialized training before 1960).

The Chinese have been critical of the quality and quantity of Soviet assistance, but some of their senior specialists have admitted that Soviet help made it possible for the Chinese to take on major scientific and technological tasks, after 1958 or 1960, without outside assistance. There were mistakes on all sides, but there is no doubt that Soviet assistance was on a massive scale and produced results that made it possible for the Chinese subsequently to adopt a policy of self-reliance without bringing their developmental programs to a halt.

Following Russia's break with China in 1960, when virtually all Russian scientists and technicians were withdrawn, Peking embarked on a policy of selective and specialized international cooperation with other nations, including non-Communist countries. The exchange programs with the Soviet Union were cut back sharply. Between 1960 and 1962, large numbers of Chinese were recalled from Russia and East Europe, leaving about two thousand—half the planned quota—in these countries. Sino-Soviet relations became increasingly strained. In June 1965, the last of the Chinese scientists, who had played a major research role, withdrew from the Joint Institute of Nuclear Research in Russia at Dubna. In the meantime, however, the Chinese scientists had been sent as early as September 1963 to the Niels Bohr Institute in Copenhagen to study atomic physics. Altogether seven Chinese scientists worked there until the last two left for home early in 1967 to participate in the Cultural Revolution.

Individual Chinese scientists began to visit and then work at European research institutes after 1961. English replaced Russian in schools as the principal foreign language. Chinese scientists, as part of Peking's technical assistance program, worked with Indonesian scientists in that country's nuclear program and other research enterprises. Between 1963 and 1966, about fifteen British scientists visited China for periods of a few weeks to as long as two years. An exchange arrangement was worked out by the Royal Society and the Chinese Academy of Sciences that provided for exchanges of students and scholars. In 1964, five Chinese were engaged in scientific research in England and by the spring of 1966 this number had grown to twenty-five.

Other exchange arrangements were worked out. The Chinese and French developed an exchange arrangement in 1964 permitting one hundred and fifty Chinese to study in France on Chinese Fellowships and thirty more with French support. Ten Chinese research fellows were also included in the arrangement that permitted, in exchange, thirty French students and ten research specialists to go to China. These plans were not fully implemented, but did begin a process of reciprocal exchange. The Canadians worked out a medical exchange lectureship with the Chi-

nese that took several prominent Canadian doctors to
China and brought two distinguished Chinese doctors to
lecture in Canada.

Australian, New Zealand, Scandinavian, Swiss, Aus-
trian, Japanese, and other scientists visited China, but no
significant pattern of scientific and scholarly exchanges
developed, although a few Chinese students and scientists
appeared in several other centers as Peking explored the
opportunities and problems of resuming intellectual and
scientific associations with non-Communist countries.
This stage was accompanied by growing cultural inter-
changes and the opening of Chinese universities to more
and more students from Europe to augment the body of
students from Afro-Asian countries, who were already
encouraged to come to China as a result of the policy of
cooperation adopted at the Bandung Conference in 1955.

In 1956, the Chinese had begun to purchase and import
large quantities of Western scientific literature. After 1960
the volume of imports increased rapidly. Chinese use of
this material appears to be reflected in their citation of
an increasing range and quantity of foreign scholarly
works in their own publications. Exchange of publication
arrangements was made between Chinese libraries and
Western university and institute libraries.

In addition, the Chinese sponsored their first major scientific conference in August 1964 at Peking. This was
clearly a political as well as a scientific undertaking for
of the 367 delegates from forty-four countries, none were
from the Soviet Union, North America, or Europe. Asia,
Africa, and Latin America were the focus of attention
in keeping with Mao's views on arenas with revolutionary potential. New Zealand and Australia came in as part
of Oceania, despite Commonwealth ties and Anzus
Treaty obligations. (For an account of this conference,
see Charles Warner, "Developing Science," *Far Eastern*

Economic Review, October 8, 1964.) Another conference
of a similar type on physics was held later in 1966. However, no Chinese scientific organizations from the Mainland belong to any of the international scientific bodies
affiliated with the International Council of Scientific Unions. Thus they are cut off from the usual international
forums for scientific discussion.

One major obstacle to Peking's participation in these
bodies is her refusal to be affiliated with any group with
representatives from Taiwan. The Nationalists understand the political importance of pre-empting the Chinese place in such bodies. This presents something of a
dilemma for scholars from the United States and other
countries who do not want to exclude Chinese from Taiwan and at the same time desire a Communist Chinese involvement in scholarly affairs. Only a few international
conferences, such as the Pugwash meetings in 1958 and
1960, have not faced the "two-China question."

Following the open conflict between China and Russia
in 1960, China began to look elsewhere for modern
equipment and industrial plant to import. Japan has
since then replaced Russia as China's largest trading part-
ner, and other countries in Europe, North America,
Oceania, and Asia have developed significant trade with
China. China, therefore, has begun to import widely di-
versified types of modern chemical, steel, and other
plant, as well as railway locomotives and aircraft, for example, from non-Communist countries. This has, of
course, fostered engineering and technical relationships
between China and these countries.

The Cultural Revolution brought many of these promising developments in scholarly and scientific relationships to an end. Over three hundred Chinese students
and researchers were recalled to China from Europe. A
few Chinese scientists and students still seem to be in

Chinese Trained in the Soviet Union, 1950-1960

CATEGORY	NUMBER	DISTRIBUTION %
Scientists[1]	1,300	3
Instructors[2]	1,200	3
Students[3]	7,500	19
Undergraduate	5,500	14
Graduate	2,000	5
Technicians[4]	8,000	21
Workers[5]	20,000	53
TOTAL[6]	38,000	100

[1] *Jen-min Jih-pao* (People's Daily), February 14, 1959, reported that 1,600 Chinese scientists went to the Soviet Union in 1959 and 1960.

[2] Between 1950 and 1958, there were 850 Chinese instructors in the USSR (*Kitai* [China] No. 4, 1960, pages 7-8; and S. L. Tikhvinskiy, "Soviet-Chinese Culture Ties," *Ten Years of the People's Republic of China*, translation in *Reports on China* series, Joint Publications Research Service [JPRS] No. 2825). In 1959, 250 Chinese instructors went to the Soviet Union (*Iz Istorii Nauki Tekhniki v Vostoka*, pages 8-33). For 1960, an estimate of only 100 was made because of the deterioration in relations between China and the Soviet Union.

[3] There were almost 7,500 Chinese students in the Soviet Union between 1950 and 1960 (M. I. Sladkovskiy, "Soviet-Chinese Economic Cooperation," *Problemy Vostokovedeniia*, translation in *Reports on China* series, JPRS No. 7155, November 29, 1960). Graduate students constituted about 25 per cent of the total.

[4] Sladkovskiy, *op. cit.*

[5] According to CKIIW, October 5, 1959, page 57, the total number of technicians and workers was 28,000. The number of workers was estimated by subtracting the number of technicians from this total.

[6] *Sinkiang Jih-pao* (Sinkiang Daily), February 14, 1960.

N.B.: Per cents may not add to total because of rounding.

Europe—a half dozen remaining in France for work in fields of high priority to the Chinese and a somewhat larger number in East Europe. The Sino-Soviet student exchanges, already sharply reduced, collapsed with the Chinese directive of September 20, 1966, by the Ministry of Higher Education instructing all foreign students to leave within fifteen days because all schools were to be closed. About fifteen Russian students were sent home and the Soviet Union, in turn, sent back sixty-five Chinese students.

Altogether several hundred foreign students in China were affected by this order. (Estimates run as follows: Albanians, 500; North Vietnamese, 200; Indonesians, 300;

Mongolians, 30; Cambodians, 20; French, 40; Bulgarians, 2; others—such as British, Swiss, Swedes, Algerians, Nepalese, Africans, Latin Americans—perhaps 100.) At the same time scholarly relationships were affected at all levels. Exchanges of publications became meaningless as over one hundred Chinese scientific journals ceased publication. Increasing numbers of visiting scholars reported that they were prevented from visiting institutions of special interest to them or of seeing Chinese specialists in their fields. Travel to China was sharply discouraged and those who once seemed to have easy access, including Edgar Snow, were reported no longer able to get into China.

At first it was believed by outside observers that the scientific and scholarly community in China would be exempt from the traumas of the Cultural Revolution. The sixteen-point charter for the Cultural Revolution, issued in August 1966, had seemingly sought to prevent disruption of scientific and technological activities in China. Article Twelve stated:

Policy toward scientists, technical personnel, and working people in general: In the course of this movement, the policy of unity—criticism—unity should be continued toward those scientists, technical personnel, and working people so long as they are patriotic and work actively without opposing the Party and Socialism, and so long as they have no improper association with foreign countries. Those scientists and technical personnel who have made contributions should be protected. Assistance may be rendered in the gradual transformation of their world outlook and work methods.

It is now clear that this has not been the case. The Academy of Sciences and its research institutes have been torn by strife. In the summer of 1967 the Red Guards had established a Revolutionary Committee in the Academy. The *People's Daily* reported reproachfully on the situation in the Academy in an editorial on July 14, 1967: "The vigorous 'civil war' among the revolutionary mass organizations lasted over twenty days, thus causing a deviation from the main orientation of the struggle." The Scientific and Technological Commission and its director, Nieh Jung-chen, have likewise been under assault. The result is that the institutions normally fostering and arranging foreign scientific relationships are in disarray and unable to function in this as in other respects. The situation is even worse with respect to student exchanges. The universities, after two years of suspension and disruption, still are not back to normal operations. A complete overhaul of the Chinese educational system has been decreed by Mao Tse-tung and this will for some time to come cripple the capacity of China to re-enter international association with other countries.

It may be wise for Communist China to temporarily cut back the goals for higher education, staked out in the first decade of their rule, in order to give more resources to the task of producing a literate public oriented toward science and elementary technological innovations. In this case, the creative capacities of China's finest minds will be frustrated and will have to preserve their talents by working in out-of-the-way corners of production-oriented institutions. The current, widespread, officially sponsored attack on intellectuals is probably not meant to damage China's talented corps of first-rate scientists who can contribute to military and industrial development, but rather it seems to be aimed at college and secondary school youths who are to be compelled to forego further studies for work in rural areas and industry where technicians are needed in large numbers. Nonetheless, Mao's latest instruction, reported in the *People's Daily* on July 21, 1968, must sound discouraging to many both inside and outside of China who hoped that modern science and technology would provide a basis for non-political global relationships. Mao's statement, as everyone in China knows, is as follows:

It is still necessary to have universities; here I refer mainly to colleges of science and engineering. However, it is essential to shorten the length of schooling, revolutionize education, put proletarian politics in command and take the road of the Shanghai Machine Tools Plant in training technicians from among the workers. Students should be selected from among workers and peasants with practical experience, and they should return to production after a few years of study.

The mood engendered by the movement of "mass technical innovations," which has been one hallmark of the Shanghai Machine Tools Plant, is not favorable to international scientific and technological relations. It is reported that at this model plant "they discard all foreign conventions and rules that limit their initiatives. The reactionary bourgeois technical 'authorities' were overthrown" ("Shanghai Industry Forges Ahead," *NCNA*, Shanghai, September 29, 1968).

After 1949, the once close association between American and Mainland Chinese students and scholars ceased. Each year about twenty thousand American scientists meet about eighty thousand foreign scientists at scholarly meetings sponsored by international scientific associations, but very few if any Chinese from the Mainland. At an informal level, however, Chinese and American scholars and scientists have occasionally exchanged communications on technical matters or have had chance meetings at conferences in third countries, particularly in those countries having diplomatic relations with Peking from which Chinese from Taiwan are barred.

No doubt there are Chinese on the Mainland who would welcome, for scientific and intellectual reasons, expanded communications with American scholars, scientists, and engineers. The National Library at Peking and the Library of the Chinese Academy of Sciences, as already noted, had developed regular exchanges of publications with major American university libraries. At one time, especially in the mid-fifties, the Chinese invited many Americans, including scholars and scientists, to visit China, but American passport regulations at that time prevented acceptance of these invitations. Since then there have been some tentative overtures indicating a desire on the part of some groups in China to develop exchanges.

Among American scholars and scientists, on the other hand, there are large numbers who would welcome direct and regular association with their Chinese counterparts. The National Academy of Sciences with the joint sponsorship of the American Council of Learned Societies and the Social Science Research Council has established a Committee on Scholarly Communications with Mainland China. Its purpose is to facilitate, if possible, improved communications for scholarly purposes.

The primary official Chinese motivations in seeking to open up channels of scholarly communication and in sending students and scientists abroad apparently have been twofold. First, they seek to benefit from training facilities in other countries that are better and more specialized than their own. Second, they seek to acquire scientific information. Much of the reporting of recent research work is contained in pre-prints. It is useful, therefore, for a specialist to be on the pre-print or Xerox circuit in his field. This exchange of reports occurs through developing personal associations with other specialists in the field. It is, of course, also advantageous for one scientist to consult and work directly with other leading scientists.

The benefits to be derived by Chinese students from

study and research in other countries unfortunately have been sharply reduced in the past by the policy of the Peking authorities of segregating Chinese abroad in their own living facilities and of restricting their freedom to mix at will with the academic community with which they are associated. This was true in Russia as it also was, for example, in France. Only mature researchers, whose political credentials are impeccable, have been allowed to work as individuals in foreign research facilities. There have been complaints that some of the young Chinese scientists abroad in the past years of testing under the Cultural Revolution have tried to demonstrate their political zeal by getting involved in embarrassing activities. This also has tended to interrupt the free flow of communications.

The foreign scientists who have visited China have been pleased, on the whole, with their reception and favorably impressed by some of the work they have observed. Even here, however, there have been restrictions on movement, on time for scholarly discussions, and on the individuals they were permitted to see. Foreign students attending Chinese universities have likewise been segregated (sometimes for good reasons) from Chinese students in special quarters and usually barred from uninhibited association with Chinese students.

Curiously, the Chinese Communists have not developed cooperative and exchange relationships with Japan in the fields of scholarship and science. Ease of handling each other's written language would facilitate exchange. Japanese scientists, many of whom have had earlier connections with China and some understanding of China's background, would seem to be an obvious source of help to the Chinese. Moreover, Japan was once a major training ground for Chinese students and even today Japan potentially provides for the Chinese a low-cost training site with excellent universities and first-rate research facilities in many fields. As it is, there is a large annual movement of visitors between China and Japan. In 1965, about seven hundred Chinese (mostly commercial and political or propaganda specialists) visited Japan and about 4,500 Japanese went for short trips to the Mainland, among them a substantial number of scholars, engineers, and professional people. This flow has been reduced but still continues. Yet the Chinese have not worked out regular arrangements to send students and researchers to Japan as they have to England, for example. The major relationship between the two countries is commercial. It may be that the Chinese believe that the political climate in Japan is potentially corrupting, that the American presence is too great, or that Taiwan's influence is too immediate and direct.

It seems unlikely that there will be a change in the Chinese policy of restricting communications and exchanges before the Cultural Revolution comes to an end. Only after a set of political leaders, with confidence in their own power and with a mature awareness of the role of science in human affairs, establishes itself again in China are there likely to be fresh decisions about the character and range of encounters between the Chinese people and outsiders. Until the political temperature is lowered and the frenzied Chinese attacks on both revisionism and capitalism moderated, few individuals or groups of scholars in China favoring expanded intellectual and other relationships with outsiders are likely to push energetically for developing such ties. It seems reasonable to assume that if China once again decides to utilize and develop all possible scientific and technological resources for modernization and developmental purposes, a new opportunity will then appear for expanding constructive intellectual and scientific relationships.

China's Nuclear Option

Michael B. Yahuda

China's achievements in the development of a nuclear
program have been impressive both in speed of progress
and variety of weapons tested. The Chinese nuclear
capability, nevertheless, is still conspicuously lacking in
delivery capability. The current Chinese nuclear strategic doctrine reflects this deficiency and nowhere envis-
ages the concept of strategic deterrence. My purpose
here is to examine the present Chinese nuclear strategic
doctrine and explore some of its political implications for
Maoist China.

In my view, once the Chinese have adopted a strategic
deterrence posture great tensions will arise in Maoist
military conceptual thinking, and indeed within the present Chinese political structure and general policies. As
deterrence involves interaction with the projected enemy, it may serve as the agent through which the Chinese
People's Republic eventually participates more fully in
the international society of states.

It is necessary first, however, to assess Chinese nuclear
development and to examine the impact of the Cultural
Revolution upon it.

Many of the more spectacular achievements of the

Chinese nuclear program came about during the Cultural Revolution. China's fourth test was of a nuclear warhead carried by a guided missile on October 27, 1966. The fifth test, of China's first thermonuclear device, took place on December 28, 1966. Her sixth was a multi-megaton H-bomb, probably dropped by an aircraft, on June 17, 1967. The speed of her nuclear development—from the first detonation of an atomic device to her first successful H-bomb test—was just over two and a half years. This was much less time than required by the other four nuclear powers. Furthermore, the Chinese overcame a wide range of technical problems to reduce the size of both their atomic and thermonuclear warheads to manageable proportions for delivery purposes.

Progress Despite Upheavals

Thus, in the early and middle phases of the Cultural Revolution, Chinese nuclear development does not seem to have been held back by the general upheavals in China. The government press communiqué on the H-bomb test did hint at some conflict among personnel on the nuclear program, and presented the test as the triumph of those who had "dared" to innovate and to improve upon "foreign methods."

Early Central Committee policy documents on the Cultural Revolution stressed that the various institutions and enterprises concerned with China's national defense program should not become involved, but toward the end of 1967 there were signs that these injunctions were no longer followed. Thus Marshal Nieh Jung-chen, head of the Science and Advanced Technology Commission and generally accepted as leader of China's nuclear development program, came under attack by Red Guards, as did General Wang Ping-chang, Minister of the Seventh Machine Building Ministry, reportedly concerned with missile development and production. Chien San-chiang, head of China's Atomic Energy Institute, was labeled a "pro-capitalist" and "secret enemy agent." Such attacks do not necessarily mean that the person concerned has been purged or demoted, although in many cases this has happened. The main effects may be in terms of the damage to the morale of those concerned and to the *esprit de corps* of the institutions in which they work.

Secret Missile Test

The Chinese conducted a nuclear test on December 24, 1967, which they did not announce—the first time this happened. It seems that this was a thermonuclear warhead on "a missile which went awry, requiring that it and its payload be destroyed prematurely," according to one report. The failure of this test need not be due to the disturbances of the Cultural Revolution. It is interesting to note that by late 1968 the Chinese had not resumed nuclear testing. Despite former U.S. Defense Secretary McNamara's prediction that the Chinese could have a first-test shot of an ICBM booster before the end of 1967, they have yet to do so. Moreover, it seems likely that the chaotic effect of the Cultural Revolution on the industrial sector of the economy, particularly the system of communications, would in any case have caused delays in delivering necessary supplies for Chinese nuclear and missile development.

It seems, however, that since late spring of 1969

the tides of the Cultural Revolution have been ebbing and that whatever dislocations may have been caused to the nuclear and missile programs, too, have ended.

Chinese Nuclear Doctrine

China, as we have seen, has not yet demonstrated a nuclear capability. This, coupled with her relatively weak air defenses, makes her nuclear installations attractive and vulnerable to aerial attack. The Chinese appear to recognize this vulnerability but claim that although such an attack would cause tremendous damage it would not defeat them. Their doctrine is, therefore, essentially defensive and is concerned with surviving a nuclear attack and ultimately defeating the attacker.

They argue that nuclear weapons can cause a great deal of damage, but that their role is limited. In the words of their Foreign Minister, Chen Yi: "The United States has been brandishing the atom bomb for atomic blackmail over the past twenty years, but it has failed." Thus, the nuclear monopoly held by the United States in the early years after World War II did not prevent Communist takeovers in East Europe and in East Asia. The "spiritual atomic bomb" of the revolutionary peoples, they argue, is far more important.

The Chinese see a nuclear attack upon them as the starting point of a general war. They expect a surprise attack which would seek to destroy at one stroke the military strength, economic centers, and major communications networks. The object would be to destroy China's will to resist, but it would fail. Because of her vast territory and huge population, China would not be destroyed. The attackers would have to follow up their nuclear strike with an armed invasion of Chinese territory, at which point the Chinese would resort to the strategy and tactics of a "people's war," which would ultimately defeat the adversary. Indeed, they anticipate that the enemy would be superior to them in the air, at sea, and in conventional fire power on the ground. Consequently, the only effective countermeasure would be to resort to a "people's war." Nuclear weapons will not replace a decisive battle by ground forces.

Certain aspects of this inherently defensive doctrine do not seem realistic, especially the premise that in the event of an American nuclear attack, the United States would find it necessary to follow this up with an armed invasion. Why the United States should not be satisfied with "taking out" certain strategic targets is not clear.

The defensive posture does, however, serve particular purposes within the present Chinese political system. First, as a doctrine of ultimate invincibility it is of great psychological value to a country under the threat of more powerful adversaries, especially since the long-term objectives and general ethos of Maoist China are directed specifically against those adversaries.

Fortress Besieged

Second, it accords well with general Maoist theory and practice. It defines a role (indeed the *decisive* role) for a people's war even in a nuclear conflict. Therefore, the Maoist concept of the role, function, and organization of the Chinese armed forces as a "people's army" not only remains valid, but is reinforced. The role of the militia is similarly enhanced: the Chinese Army must continue as a "people's army" pursuing Maoist objectives rather than emphasizing a purely military outlook associated with the highly professionalized and exclusive officer corps of conventional armies.

The implications of this doctrine for Maoist practice clearly extend beyond the military sphere to embrace nearly all aspects of political culture. Chinese leaders regard China today as a fortress of socialism under siege, as "the center of world revolution," the survival of which is necessary and vital to the cause of revolutionary forces throughout the world. The appeal of this doctrine, in this context, is obvious, but such a perspective does suggest that the Chinese feel vulnerable to nuclear attack and that their nuclear program is designed to close a gap in their defenses.

Chinese thinking on nuclear strategy seems somewhat superficial. The role of nuclear weapons in the conflict scenario they envisage seems more in the nature of an artillery barrage to soften up the enemy before the attack than the carefully selected targets on the rungs of Herman Kahn's ladder of escalation. This apparent lack of sophistication may be a function of the stage they have reached in their nuclear development. In any case it reflects their views on the role of nuclear weapons as well as their reasons for "going nuclear." Briefly these may be said to be three related factors:

1. The quest for superpower status, which has both negative and positive dimensions. The negative is concerned with how others view China. As Chen Yi once remarked, "capitalists consider us underdeveloped and defenseless as long as we lack the ultimate weapons." The positive dimension is concerned with the Chinese wish to effect political change in the world more to their liking, by supporting friends or threatening enemies. They have already taken tentative steps in these directions, first, by claiming after each of their tests that these

have "encouraged" revolutionaries abroad, particularly the Vietnamese and the Arabs; and second, by uttering threats to the Japanese after China's first test to the effect that "if [U.S. imperialism] starts a [nuclear] war, Japan, as a U.S. nuclear base, is bound to bear the brunt and will inevitably be pushed into the abyss of nuclear calamity." The threat was made in the context of an attack on the Japanese government for permitting the landing of American nuclear submarines in Japan. China did not have the capability to deliver its A-bomb on target and the threat, therefore, lacked credibility. The Chinese do not appear to have made similar threats after 1964, but the fact that they made them at all would suggest that they do see superpower status in positive terms.

2. The view of their nuclear program as a symbol of "self-reliance," and as a means through which they hope to acquire an advanced technology.

3. The need to fill a gap in China's national defense. Economically, China is virtually self-sufficient, and she would not be unduly hurt by naval action. Therefore, she has little to fear from action at sea. She probably has even less to fear from a physical invasion of her territory by conventional armies, but she is acutely vulnerable from the air. Given the Chinese view of themselves as a fortress of socialism under siege, a major goal must be to make the fortress invulnerable. The Chinese nuclear program seems designed to meet this objective.

However, as we have seen, there is little to suggest that they have spelled out exactly how their nuclear program will give them invulnerability. There is, in short, no distinct nuclear strategy toward which the Chinese are known to be working. One way in which we may be able to discern more clearly how they expect their nuclear program to meet this objective is to examine more closely the options available to them in acquiring a nuclear delivery system and the available evidence suggesting which option they will choose.

Delivery Options

The availability of options is obviously dependent upon China's level of technological development, particularly in the areas vital for missiles and guidance systems. There is very little information publicly available on this, and often that little is based upon inference. Furthermore, the options the Chinese choose (or have already chosen) will also be determined by the political and strategic objectives they have set themselves. Ideally, another factor which would govern their decisions would be the strategies and capabilities of their enemies or potential enemies in a few year's time, when the Chinese delivery system becomes operational.

The options available to the Chinese are: (1) the long-range manned bomber aircraft; (2) medium-range ballistic missiles (MRBMs) and intermediate-range ballistic missiles (IRBMs), any of which could be tailored to a procurement of long-range submarines capable of launching missiles, as well as being launched from ground bases; and (3) intercontinental missiles (ICBMs) with a range of several thousand miles.

Since the Chinese are not developing a program of producing long-range bombers, they appear to have rejected the first option.

The second option has much to recommend it in Chinese eyes. It is within their technical competence: their fourth test, over two years ago, was of a nuclear warhead of low-yield kiloton fired by a guided missile over a distance of about four hundred miles. (It was probably based on the Russian "Komet" missile—but the Chinese did adapt and fire it and could do so again.) The drain on their resources, both of the requisite material supplies and in terms of cost, would be less than an ICBM-based delivery system.

Furthermore, the technical problems in the development, production, and operation of MRBMs and IRBMs are far less than those of ICBMs; in fact, more could be produced and stockpiled. But perhaps most significantly, this option could be made operational more speedily—probably even before the early 1970s when the American ABM system comes into operation. Should the Chinese also tailor this to the production of long-range submarines capable of launching these missiles they would conceivably have the ability to counter some aspects of the ABM system at a relatively low cost to themselves. It could well be, however, that the development of a sufficiently powerful and competent naval force to sustain such a strategy might be too costly or demanding on their industrial and personnel resources.

Main Targets

The main strategy which would follow from taking the MRBM-IRBM option would be essentially regional. The main targets presumably would be those countries on China's periphery who were allied with or sympathetic to the United States and especially those which had U.S. bases on their territory. The political objectives underlying such targeting would be to induce the decline and perhaps removal of American influence from the area of South, Southeast, and East Asia. Initially, the objectives could be to have a further lever by which to impose limits to local wars in the area and to provide "cover" to revolutionary wars. It would open to the Chinese various opportunities to indulge in nuclear diplomacy and play a more dominant role in the political conflicts in the area.

Whether it could be used as a deterrent to the United States from attacking China is more doubtful, for two reasons: the Chinese would need to demonstrate that they had a second-strike capability, and, perhaps more importantly, this area of Asia is not of the same importance to the Americans as West Europe. The strategy which the Soviets used in the 1950s to deter the United States by threatening West Europe may not in fact work for the Chinese in Asia. While it may increase Chinese influence in Asia it would not necessarily provide China with the capability to adopt a deterrence posture toward the United States.

Much would depend upon the role the United States would define for itself in Asia in such a situation, and upon the reactions of the relevant Asian countries. At this juncture no predictions can be made as the variables involved are many and complex, particularly if the Chinese were to adopt such a strategy before the American ABM system became operational.

The adoption of such a strategy by China may indeed prove counterproductive, especially regarding Japan and India. Both have the know-how and the capacity to go nuclear. Such a Chinese strategy may well drive them to procure a nuclear capability. Should the pattern for the future be one of even partial withdrawal of American commitment to the area, this course of action would seem inevitable for the two countries. Although initially the Chinese would enjoy an advantage it is likely that the Japanese, particularly, would catch up and overtake them. For some time, too, the Chinese would enjoy a geographical advantage. The Sino-Indian borders are far closer to strategic Indian targets (within easy MRBM and IRBM range) than are the Chinese equivalents (more within ICBM range). Similar considerations apply to the Sino-Japanese sector. The disparity is not great, but the relevant Japanese strategic centers are more concentrated and less diffuse than is the case with China. Nevertheless, as McNamara once remarked, "a relatively small number of warheads detonated over fifty Chinese cities would destroy half the urban population and more than half of the prized industrial capacity."

A further consideration for China is that the MRBM-IRBM option would be unlikely to effect the recovery of Taiwan. Nuclear weapons are hardly the means with which to settle a civil war. They could be used to deter a projected invasion force from Taiwan. But, in view of the whole Maoist ethos and policies, the use of nuclear weapons for such a purpose seems so unlikely that it would serve to undermine the efficacy and application of the doctrine of "people's war" and much that stems from it in terms of army-building and social structures.

The Appeal of ICBMs

The third option—an ICBM-based strategy—would be the most satisfying psychologically to the present Chinese leadership and to Mao in particular. At one fell stroke, the Chinese would have acquired the most advanced weapon, the multi-megaton warhead, and the most advanced means of delivery, the ICBM. The American mainland would be within its range as indeed would the Urals and European Russia. Chinese leadership could claim that any part of the world was within range of their missiles.

The technical problems in achieving an operational ICBM are very great, as are indeed its demands upon money, resources, and qualified personnel. It has been estimated that current Chinese defense expenditure is about ten per cent of China's GNP. The cost of her nuclear establishment has been estimated at two per cent of the GNP. Two points are important in this context. First, the proportion of China's most skilled and technically advanced personnel engaged on this project must be very large—with a consequent loss to other sectors of industry. Second, as a proportion of central government disposal income, the expenditure on nuclear and missile development must also be much greater than the two per cent GNP would indicate. The number of ICBMs the Chinese would be capable of producing annually would, on estimates of her current capacity, be fewer than ten. The deployment and targeting would have to be sophisticated so as to pierce the American ABM screen. It would be very costly and it would be far from certain whether China could inflict unacceptable damage on a first-strike basis, not to mention a second-strike capability, which they could surely not procure before the 1980s. The temptation for the United States to launch a pre-emptive strike in any crisis situation would be very great. Therefore, Chinese vulnerability would increase substantially for the first few years.

Current, although incomplete, evidence suggests that the Chinese are striving for an ICBM capability. They have MRBMs, but there is no evidence of deployment. Perhaps they may be aiming initially for a capability that involves a combination of both options. The testing of a few ICBMs would be prestigious and may bring psychological-political gains, but the main core of their delivery system could still be MRBM-IRBM-based. An alternative would be to stress an exclusively anti-American capability which would involve primarily ICBMs, but also MRBMs and IRBMs targeted at local U.S. bases.

Deterrence Posture

At no point since 1949 has China become a full participatory member of the international committee of nations, a fact symbolized by her exclusion from the United Nations, but one that extends far beyond that. Her relatively isolated position stems in part from American containment policies, but increasingly in the 1960s it has been reinforced by Chinese postures and policies. In the 1950s, China was a member of the Soviet "socialist commonwealth," and the bulk of her trade and cultural relations, as well as her international political orientations, lay with the Soviet Union and East Europe. In the mid-fifties a further area of interest developed with the Afro-Asian countries, but the level of interest here, too, seemed to drop after 1964, although friendly relations with a few of these countries are still maintained.

The main drive of Chinese policies in the 1960s has been toward "self-reliance," which involves becoming dependent exclusively upon Chinese internal resources and cutting back any dependence on outside countries. This has extended beyond the economic to include the cultural and political spheres. The Chinese leaders, especially the Maoists, argue that the only basis for true authority in the world today is the "thought of Mao Tse-tung." While the Chinese claim the right to disseminate his "thought" universally, they do not allow reciprocal rights in China. Chinese leadership appears willing to countenance only those views and perspectives which fit their particularist doctrine.

Chinese isolation is not as clear-cut as suggested above, for even the vagaries of Red Guard diplomacy in 1966-67 did not impair friendly Sino-Pakistan relations, for example. This particular relationship (like several others) seems to be based on certain strategic considerations, notably their respective relations with India. Nevertheless, the direction of Chinese policies toward greater exclusiveness and "self-reliance" is unmistakable. This may change in the future as the result of various possible factors, notably the death of Mao. But the Chinese have a long history of isolationism and this aspect of Maoist China could conceivably outlast the passing of the "Mao era."

One way in which this pattern of exclusiveness may be changed could arise out of China's adaptation of a deterrence posture. Deterrence is not so much concerned with the actual use of particular weapons but with the threat to use them. Strategic deterrence involves a process of interaction with the adversary, which necessitates minimally a two-way communication of intentions, capabilities, and, beyond that, policies and strategies. The communications need not be perfect in terms of clarity and certainty in all these spheres but they must be in some of them.

This process of interaction, in the initial stages, may be very limited. To a certain extent the bilateral Sino-American ambassadorial talks in Warsaw indicate that this process has been going on for a long time without arresting the trend toward isolation. These talks do indicate, however, that Chinese exclusiveness is already incomplete, and with the advent of nuclear deterrence strategy will be further broken.

The evidence that does exist concerning Chinese "rationality" in terms of risk-taking points to the fact that the Chinese have so far shown themselves to be quite rational in the calculation of the risks to their national security arising out of their own actions, notably in the Sino-Indian border war, in the Taiwan straits and off-shore islands, and in the current Vietnam war. Therefore, there seems no *a priori* reason to argue that the Chinese leaders would not learn the rules of deterrence. Chinese deployment of a strategic deterrence capability may indeed serve as the primary agency by which China becomes inducted into fuller participatory membership in the international community of states in more ways than by simply sitting on certain international bodies, such as the U.N. Security Council.

The Five Principles—
A New Approach

Merry Selk

The first big power to approach the Nixon administration—even before it took office—was the People's Republic of China. On November 26, in a Peking Radio broadcast, the Chinese Foreign Ministry announced it had proposed a meeting with the new administration's representatives on February 20 in Warsaw to discuss the "Five Principles of Coexistence."

China has called for diplomatic discussion of the "Five Principles" in the mid-fifties and again in the early sixties, but the call has not been repeated in Chinese communications of the last several years.

"The Five Principles of Coexistence" are probably those outlined by China in 1955: respect for territorial integrity and sovereignty; nonaggression; noninterference in the internal affairs of other states; equality and mutual benefit and peaceful coexistence.

The meeting proposed by the Chinese would be the one hundred and thirty-fifth diplomatic exchange between China and the United States. Each side has accused the other of being responsible for the lapse between the previous meeting—January 8, 1968—and the proposed February date. The United States suggested meetings in May and in September, which were "postponed" when there was no official Chinese response to the suggestions.

The Chinese proposal is apparently a trial balloon to test the Nixon administration's willingness to alter the United States' policy toward China. The President's indications of a preferential interest in Europe rather than Asia do not rule out the possibility of change.

This tentative Chinese proposal has led some China experts to speculate further on developments in Chinese internal politics which may have precipitated the move at this time. Some experts infer that the Chinese internal situation has thawed. They cite a contrast between bellicose Chinese foreign policy statements in the last two years and the relative mildness of this proposal, which is at variance with the Chinese policy of diplomatic isolation in the last several years. The proposal also stands out in contrast to Cultural Revolutionary pressure on foreign diplomats and attacks on foreign embassies in Peking. It should be recalled also that two earlier meetings with the United States were postponed.

A Détente with the West?

There is a suggestion here of an ending of the Cultural Revolution or at least of its influence in foreign policy. Is it possible that China is probing a relationship with the United States as a backstop against further deterioration of its already tense relations with the Soviet Union? China has increased its troop allocations on the Sino-Soviet border. If military action portends there, China would not want a hostile power on her seaward flank, where the United States Seventh Fleet patrols.

A French commentator, Phillipe Ben, in *Le Monde*, contends that the Chinese proposal must be seen in the context of United States-Russian relations. He suggests that Chinese pressure on the eastern border of the Soviet Union was a factor in the Russian invasion of Czechoslovakia to strengthen the western border. Is the Chinese proposal, then, a move to counter a Soviet-American détente?

Both China and the Soviet Union seem to view an entente by the other with the United States as a threat. One may argue, for example, that China would be unlikely to develop an understanding with the United States unless Soviet-American relations were deteriorating. The Soviets, on their part, noted the Chinese November 26 proposal with displeasure.

The likely end of the war in Vietnam is recognized as another factor which may have influenced the Chinese announcement. If the war is ending and a settlement is negotiated, China may be indicating her interest in influencing the terms. The Vietnam war has been threatening to China. American bombers have strayed over its territory, and it has been justified as containing Chinese expansionism. Perhaps, then, the Chinese proposal reflects an interest in cooling the Southeast Asian situation to leave China free for internal development. Whatever Vietnam settlement is advanced, it seems clear that it could call for a new rationale for the United States' China policy.

The Chinese November 26 proposal is not an abstraction. It has meaning, as one observer remarked, only if the offer is part of a process: only if the United States responds.

President Richard M. Nixon has assumed office at a time when new initiatives in world politics are essential. Chiang Kai-shek's elder son, Defense Minister Chiang

Ching-kuo, has admitted that reconquest of the mainland is "a dream." More informal meetings between the United States and China, a relaxation of the trade embargo or of restrictions on private travel to both countries, might be the results of less hostile relations between Peking and Washington.

But the Nixon administration's policy on China is, so far, not clear. It is difficult to estimate what will be possible within Nixon's own viewpoint and that of his entourage. It is clear that as long as the United States' approach to its China policy is one of response, Washington will always be responding on other countries' terms to what happens in China and Southeast Asia.

SCIENCE AND
TECHNOLOGY

Science Travels the Mao Road

C. H. G. Oldham

For only two of the nineteen years that have elapsed since the foundation of the People's Republic of China—from mid-1964 to mid-1966—has it been relatively easy for the Westerner (though not the American) to visit China. I visited China twice during this time. My first visit was for a month in 1964, and the second was in 1965 when I traveled from Hong Kong to London by train, with my wife and four children.

In addition to informal visits by tourists, including several scientists, formal scientific exchanges between China and several Western countries took place during this period. There were, for example, scientific exchanges between the Royal Society and the Chinese Academy of Sciences, and between the French and Chinese governments. Scientists from a number of other countries went to China on official visits.

At this time there was also a flourishing exchange of scientific journals. Scientific visitors to China almost invariably commented on the excellence of Chinese collections of foreign journals, and many noted the up-to-date knowledge of international science on the part of their Chinese colleagues. The quality of Chinese scientific publications had steadily improved and by 1965 at least three of their journals were translated into English. The general impression gained both from the journals and from the visits of foreign scientists was that the caliber of Chinese research was sound, but that few spectacular breakthroughs had been made, or seemed likely to be made in the near future.

Then, in mid-1966, the Cultural Revolution began and international contacts were broken off. So far as I know, no Chinese scientific journals have been received in Britain since October 1966, and I suspect none has been published in China since that date. A Royal Society exchange was suspended in the autumn of 1966 and since then few Western scientists have visited China. In fact the only sources of information about science in China today are the official Chinese press reports and broadcasts.

Fortunately, both the American Consulate in Hong Kong and the BBC monitoring service in Caversham provide transcripts of the most significant of the Chinese daily press statements and broadcasts, so that even without a detailed knowledge of the Chinese language it is possible to keep informed about some of the activities in China today. The information which these sources provide about science is scanty, and all of it reflects the views of those in China who are loyal to Mao Tse-tung. Nevertheless, it does provide a tantalizing glimpse of recent events and policies.

Liu Supporters

One of the first statements about science and the Cultural Revolution came in the communiqué issued by the

Central Committee of the Chinese Communist Party
in August 1966. This communiqué said in part that scientists and technologists were to be excluded from the
rigors of the Cultural Revolution. Apparently the Party
recognized that although many scientists still did not
fully support Mao Tse-tung, their work was so important
to the country that they should be given special consideration. From reports in the Chinese press it now seems
that this policy has not been honored. At the time of the
communiqué most of the leaders in the Academy of Sciences, the foremost scientific body in China, appeared
to be loyal to the President of the Republic, Liu Shao-chi.
During much of the autumn of that year and the following spring, there were attempts on the part of the pro-
Mao scientists to seize power from the pro-Liu group.
At times fighting broke out in some of the research institutes, especially those in Peking and Tsinan, but most
of the real trouble seems to have been among rival groups
all of which claimed to be supporters of Mao Tse-tung.

The main scientific crimes of Liu Shao-chi and his supporters were announced at a large rally held in Peking
in April 1967. On that occasion representatives of the
Revolutionary Rebels of the Chinese Academy of Sciences accused the supporters of Liu of promoting research
which was aimed at restoring what was ancient and wor-
shipping what was foreign. They had advocated research
that was theoretical and divorced from the needs of the
country. They were also accused of supporting titles such
as "professor," and finally they had called for high sal-
aries for scientists and awards for those who had made
special contributions. By implication, the pro-Mao group
opposed these policies.

Then, three months later, a grand rally of all the proletarian revolutionaries of the Chinese Academy of Sciences was held in the Great Hall of the People in Peking.

The rally supposedly marked the seizure of power from Liu Shao-chi's supporters and the formation of a new Revolutionary Committee, which was to be the organ of power in the Academy. Two things are significant about the constitution of this committee. First, representatives of the People's Liberation Army sit on it, so the military are now in a position to exercise some control over civil science. Second, two of the members are Chu Ko-chan and Wu Yu-hsun, both of whom have been vice-presidents of the Academy for many years, so that despite the reported upheavals, they, together with Kuo Mo-jo, the president of the Academy, have all maintained their former positions of leadership. Indeed, it is difficult to determine just how much damage has been done to science during the Cultural Revolution. Some projects which had been shelved by Liu Shao-chi's supporters have been restored now that the pro-Mao group has authority. For example, a large new radio telescope was recently completed. Work on this began in 1958, but was stopped when the pro-Liu group gained control. It was rushed to completion in time for the period of intense solar activity in 1968.

Another notable recent achievement of the Academy was a major scientific expedition to Mount Everest: one hundred scientists from thirty scientific disciplines took part in a comprehensive survey covering a large area. Other accomplishments of the research institutes of the Chinese Academy of Sciences recently reported in Chinese newspapers include the discovery of a new fossil skullcap of Peking Man at Choukoutien, and the construction of a new all-purpose transistorized digital computer.

Arguments over research priorities, and even struggles for power within research institutes, are not unique to China: what is unique is the requirement that scientists should use the writings of Mao Tse-tung, not only as a guide to correct ideological thinking, but also as a research tool. All the announcements of innovations contain tributes to the influence of Mao's writings. But despite the enormous amount of time that must be devoted to the study of Mao, it is unlikely that this causes much harm to scientific work. Those quotations which are most frequently cited by scientists amount to nothing more than little truisms recognized as valid by any research scientist. There is nothing wrong with "Don't be overawed by the authorities in science—always be willing to challenge their beliefs."

Meeting National Goals

In addition to disputes over the policies for science, there have also been disputes over the way science should be used to meet national goals. Consider military research. The decision to build an atomic bomb was probably taken in 1958. It was opposed by supporters of Liu Shao-chi on the grounds that it would be a waste of China's resources. Reliance on the Soviet Union was urged instead. An article in the *Peking Review* said that two roads lay before the Chinese people: they could either catch up with other countries by bold new creations and embarking on a road no man has trodden before (the Mao road), or they could model themselves on the West and crawl slowly forward (the Liu road). Whether Chinese scientists did succeed in pioneering a "bold new creation" in nuclear technology is still open to speculation. The Chinese themselves have been extremely reticent to provide any sort of technical information about their bombs. From the official statements, we know only that seven

atomic explosions have taken place, and that at least
one of these was a hydrogen bomb. We also know that
a guided missile was launched successfully—but we know
neither its warhead capacity nor its range.

But analysis of the radioactive fallout associated with
the bombs showed that they were made from U-235 and
not plutonium, as had generally been expected. This
raises some interesting questions. The separation of U-235
from the more abundant U-238 isotope is a difficult feat
which requires a physical rather than a chemical technology. Two methods have been used by Western countries:
an electro-magnetic separation technique and a method
based on gaseous diffusion. It was assumed that gaseous
diffusion would have been the logical choice in China,
but this requires large amounts of electrical energy and
a very large plant. American intelligence claimed to have
located a possible gaseous-diffusion plant near Lanchow,
but this seemed too small to be able to produce the
amount of U-235 needed for the bombs so far exploded.

A number of alternative speculations have been made.
The one which is gaining ground is that Chinese scientists have perfected another technique based on the principle of a gas centrifuge. The evidence for this is still frag-
mentary, but Chinese scientists are known to have been
working on it at least as early as 1961. Also the fact that
Dutch scientists have recently succeeded with this method
shows that it is feasible.

A second area of serious conflict between Mao and Liu
concerns the choice of technology in agriculture. On the
problem of mechanization in Heilungkiang Province,
for instance, both Mao Tse-tung and Liu Shao-chi agree
that in the long run agricultural methods must be mech-
anized to the maximum possible extent. They differ only
on the strategy to be followed in achieving this objective.
Liu Shao-chi said that because there were insufficient

tractors to go around they should be deployed in the most economically efficient manner. He attacked the Mao policy of encouraging each Commune to have its own tractor station and advocated the setting up of state "ploughing companies." These could own the tractors, employ experts, and provide contract service giving priority to those Communes which have a large acreage and a shortage of draught animals. For advocating such a policy Liu Shao-chi was accused of pragmatism, and of putting economic factors before political ones.

Mao Tse-tung's policy is to encourage self-reliance at all levels. He believes that the best way to transform society is to encourage everyone to innovate. So, he says, those Communes which can afford tractors should use them. He goes further and suggests that the best way to reach the ultimate objective of agricultural mechanization is to adopt the famous "walking on two legs" policy. Under it, the most modern techniques are to be adopted as soon as and wherever possible, but in the meantime, less modern and more labor-intensive innovations are encouraged. This policy difference is also reflected in attitudes toward research in agricultural mechanization. Liu wanted to concentrate the provinces' scientific resources in a few advanced centers. But Mao favored setting up "dozens" of semi-mechanization research institutes which would carry out research on intermediate-level technologies. If economic development is the sole objective, the policies ascribed to Liu are probably correct. If total development is the goal, and greater importance is attached to social and political factors, then Mao's policies make good sense.

Educational Differences

But the sharpest and perhaps most significant differences between Mao and Liu have been centered on their
educational policies. The nineteen-year period of Communist rule in China has been characterized by two
educational trends. One is a continuing emphasis on scientific and technical education. The other is an alternating
policy of greater and then lesser emphasis on political and
ideological education.

My first visit to Chinese universities and schools coin-
cided with a period when Liu's supporters controlled
educational policies. The emphasis at that time was on
quality and expertise and there was a minimum of concern with politics. Now it is this policy which is condemned.

Liu Shao-chi and his supporters are accused of setting
up a system of elite schools throughout each of the provinces. Roughly a quarter of all schools were singled
out for special support, and in order to get to the better
universities it was necessary to have graduated from one
of these "key schools." It is now claimed that this system
promoted elitism, and the whole policy, remarkably
similar to the old British system of secondary education,
is thoroughly condemned.

One institute of higher education that has been singled out for especially bitter attack is the Peking Medical
College. This college had an eight-year course and trained
the best doctors in China. However, the latest attacks
claim that the courses were too intensive, and too many
irrelevant facts had to be learned. When the doctors

graduated they were so specialized and so dependent on expensive equipment that when they came to practice medicine "they were like cripples without crutches." Even a case of plagiarism by one of the professors is cited as an example of the college's corrupt bourgeois ways.

The present emphasis is on a totally different form of education with drastically curtailed courses. To enable the new courses to be designed and to release the students for Red Guard activities, Mao closed the schools and universities in mid-1966. They were supposed to reopen a year later but many didn't. Last autumn one of the principal slogans in the Chinese press was: "Resume classes to make revolution." But judging by the continued exhortation to the students this spring to return to class, it would seem that many are still absent. In fact this refusal to resume class may indicate the first genuine student revolt since the Cultural Revolution began.

It is still not clear what the new education policy is going to be, but the educational innovations introduced by Tung-chi University in Shanghai are being promulgated as an example for others to copy. This was one of the foremost technological universities in China but its course has been cut from five years to three and the teaching function has been combined with design and production work. Only about half to two-thirds of the students' time is spent in the classroom. It is claimed that the new type of education is much more in line with what is needed for a country in China's state of development, and that the theory which is taught is more closely related to production requirements. The major curriculum reforms, combined with policies which reserve nearly all the university places for the children of peasants and workers, are bound to have profound implications for China's development.

Some Progress

It is, I think, clear that scientific institutions and scientists have been caught up in the turmoil and confusion which characterize China today. Nevertheless, announcements continue to be made of new scientific and technological achievements. For example, in addition to the well-known nuclear successes, scientists and engineers have recently synthesized insulin, produced the world's first synthetic benzine plant, made an automated pure oxygen top-blown steel converter, and made a new double light-beam infrared spectrophotometer and an automatic stereo camera.

However, it must be recognized that these are isolated successes. A Japanese assessment recently put China ten to fifteen years behind Japan in most areas of technology. China's own target in science, announced in January 1966, was to catch up with the advanced countries within twenty to thirty years. Before the Cultural Revolution there was a good possibility of this goal being reached. Now, priorities have been changed and there is less likelihood of this happening across a wide scientific front. But the new policies will probably result in a greater concentration of scientific relevance to China's development needs. And this is a policy which I would myself endorse.

A Reader's Guide to Publications from and on China

Richard Harris and
William Brugger

Short histories of modern China and the Chinese revolution are now becoming commonplace. Some aim no higher than the school textbook and tend to be colorless. One of the latest that is well-informed, politically involved, and always concentrates on the essentials is *China: Empire to People's Republic* by George Moseley. Half the space goes to the end of the Old China and the Kuomintang interregnum, with light thrown on such pivotal moments as the May 4 movement. From this background the rise of Communism falls naturally into place in the second part. Such themes as the Sino-Soviet alliance and dispute, the crucial issue of Taiwan, and Mao Tse-tung's rejection of Russian economic methods in favour of his own mass line are emphasized.

While Mr. Moseley's running theme is revolution, *The Modern History of China* (Weidenfeld, London, 1967) gains enormously from the late Henry McAleavy's experience of life in China under Kuomintang and Communist rule. A specialist in the Manchus and an author with a great appreciation of social and cultural interaction, McAleavy gives us the bones of modern Chinese political change while clothing it with sentient flesh.

Such histories written from a distance need filling out with a recent close-up. Dick Wilson wrote his general survey of revolutionary China, *Anatomy of China* (Weybright & Talley, New York, 1967, $8.50), after a tour of the country in 1964 when recovery from the confusion of the Great Leap Forward was plain to see. After some years studying China in Hong Kong, Mr. Wilson gives us a lucid analysis of the economy and comes to grips with the popular revolution. Moreover he is incisive enough to face such questions as Tibet—freedom or progress? Much of his subject matter has a new relevance today under the impact of the Cultural Revolution.

No doubt many studies of that tornado of individual struggle are now in press. The early stages were by chance observed by many young Sinologists from Britain, Australia, and France who had been recruited, in the years before the Cultural Revolution began, to teach English and French. Colin McKerras and Neale Hunter were two such Australians whose *China Observed* is lively and readable. It conveys the excitement of the experience and gains from the revolutionary curiosity and sympathy that many of these young Sinologists shared. Unlike political tourists who write so many ephemeral books on China, these men could talk to the people and read the posters. Hans Granqvist's *The Red Guard* (Pall Mall, $4.20) is another visiting journalist's view.

The latest book on the Cultural Revolution belongs to that rare species of major writers taking an interest in China. Alberto Moravia does this with great effect in *The Red Book* and *The Great Wall* (Secker & Warburg, London, 1968, $3). He seizes on the noble revolutionary indigence at the heart of Mao Tse-tung's values and round this he builds many other surprising insights on the nature of the Chinese in general and as observed in

the Cultural Revolution. The book is immensely readable. While never leaving his European liberal standpoint, Moravia yet contrives to feel his way into all the
realities of China's upheaval. Jules Roy, the French
writer, made his *Journey to China* (Faber & Faber, London, 1967, $5) before the Cultural Revolution. Tourist
management and Communist bureaucracy were too much
for him; his serious penetration of events fell short of his
hopes but his travel diary has its liveliness and irritated
comprehension of the way Chinese behave toward foreign
visitors.

Collections of documents and analysis of the Sino-
Soviet dispute have been rather overshadowed by the
pullulating changes of the Cultural Revolution. Nevertheless John Gittings' *Survey of the Sino-Soviet Dispute*
has the virtue of taking the quarrel subject by subject
and quoting not only what was said about the matter
during the dispute but what had been said before when
relations were supposed to be good. This brings out the
pith of the argument very effectively and Mr. Gittings'
own annotations are admirably done.

At the heart of this dispute of course and of the Cultural Revolution during the last three years are the personality and the obsessions of Mao Tse-tung. Stuart
Schram's outstanding biography, *Mao Tse-tung* (Pen-
guin, London, 1967 $6), has been twice revised since
it was first published in 1966. It is a most penetrating
analysis of the development of this quirky, unrelenting
devotee of revolution, revolution, and always revolution.
Mao has so dominated the scene in China that the history of the People's Republic in the twenty years since
the Communist takeover might almost be regarded as a
counterpoint between Mao and the rest of his colleagues. In the Cultural Revolution itself a narrow and

rather significant selection of thoughts from the Chairman have been made into a talisman for all young revolutionaries. Stuart Schram has also reproduced these *Quotations from Chairman Mao Tse-tung* (Pall Mall, London, $5), together with his own political and bibliographical analysis, showing the motives behind the selection, the sometimes misleading sources, and the effect on the simple reader which the quotations aim to produce.

While a biography of Mao is one way of understanding what has been happening in China these last twenty years there is really no substitute for discovering as well how the country has been organized and to what revolutionary purposes. What has the revolution meant for the peasant? What role is played by the Communist cadre? For the answer to questions like these there is no substitute for Franz Schurmann's *Ideology and Organization in Communist China* (University of California Press, 1966, $12.50), a book that takes the revolution seriously at its own valuation, sifts its real achievements, and often gets to the heart of the matter—though not without exacting from the reader the passage of some thickets of jargon.

Matching this in its knowledge and with the added advantage of a long personal experience of China is Jacques Guillermaz's *Histoire du Parti Communiste Chinois, 1921–49*. M. Guillermaz was a military attaché in China both before and since the Communist government but his history is well grounded in the political and cultural background as well as the important military factors in the Communist rise to power.

For the most recent developments in China a useful source would be the three volumes of *China in Crisis*, the papers read at conferences on China at the University of Chicago, 1966 and 1967, edited by Ho Ping-ti and Tang Tsou. Some concentrate directly on the questions raised by the Cultural Revolution, others throw light on it in historical perspective and from specialized angles such as the economic.

Finally for those who like to think of China as a civilization that is bound to come out of its decades of revolution no more unrecognizable than was the France of 1820 from the France of 1789, a stimulating book is François Geoffroy-Dechaume's sensitive study, *China Looks at the World* (Faber & Faber, London, 1967, $4.50). Arranged partly as a series of letters to a Chinese friend, partly as an exploration of Chinese modes in various aspects of life, and partly as a consideration of the underlying character of revolution in China, it is based on many years of living in China and on its periphery, including a recent spell in the French Embassy in Peking.

Other recommended titles that fill out some of the themes mentioned above are:

John E. Rue. *Mao Tse-tung in Opposition*. Stanford University Press, 1967, $11.

John Gittings. *The Role of the Chinese Army*. Oxford, 1967, $6.

A. Doak Barnett. *Cadres, Bureaucracy and Political Power in Communist China*. Allen & Unwin, London, $10.

Audrey Donnithorne. *China's Economic System*. Allen & Unwin, London, $10.

Franz Schurmann (ed.). *China Readings* (3 vols. in paperback giving extracts covering the last century's history and the current revolution).

Dennis Bloodworth. *Chinese Looking Glass*. Secker & Warburg, London, 1967, $4.50.

Robert Trumbull (ed.). *This is Communist China*. David McKay, New York, 1968, $5.95.

C. R. Hensman. *China: Yellow Peril? Red Hope?* S. C. M. Press, London, 1968, $3.50.

K. S. Karol. *China: The Other Communism.* Heinemann, London, 1967, $8.40.

Jack Gray and Patrick Cavendish. *Chinese Communism in Crisis.* Pall Mall, London, 1968, $4.80.

Han Suyin. *Birdless Summer.* Cape, London, 1968, $4.20.

Notes on Contributors

W. A. C. ADIE is senior research fellow in Far Eastern Studies at St. Antony's College, Oxford. He was previously employed by the British Foreign Office as an expert in Far Eastern affairs. He is the co-author of several books on Sino-Soviet affairs and has published numerous articles on Chinese foreign policy and internal affairs in such journals as *International Affairs* and *China Quarterly*.

WILLIAM BRUFFER is materials officer at the Contemporary China Institute of the School of Oriental and African Studies in London.

ROBERT F. DERNBERGER is associate professor of economics and a member of the Center for Chinese Studies at the University of Michigan.

C. P. FITZGERALD is professor emeritus of Far Eastern history, Australian National University, Canberra. He lived in China from 1923 to 1939, working during the latter part of that period at Tali, in Yunnan Province, under a fellowship for anthropological research; and again from 1946 to 1950, as a representative of the British Council in North China. He has subsequently visited China twice, in 1956 and 1958. He is the author of numerous books, including *China: A Short Cultural History* (1935, 1961, paperback, 1965), *The Third China* (1965), and *The Chinese View of Their Place in the World* (1964 and 1966).

JOHN GITTINGS is an assistant editor of the *Far Eastern Economic Review*. He was previously on the staff of the Royal Institute of International Studies, Chile. His publications include *The Role of the Chinese Army*, 1967, and *Survey of the Sino-Soviet Dispute*, 1968.

JACK GRAY is senior lecturer in Chinese Studies at the University of Glasgow and a former lecturer at Hong Kong University; he visited the Chinese mainland in 1955. He is co-author of *Chinese Communism in Crisis*, 1968, and author of the forthcoming book, *Revolution and Consolidation in the Chinese Countryside, 1947-56*.

RICHARD HARRIS is deputy foreign editor and Far Eastern specialist of *The London Times*. From 1947-50 he served in the British Embassy information department in Tientsin and Shanghai, and was the *Times* correspondent first in Hong Kong and then in Singapore. Based in London since 1955, he visited China in 1954 and again in 1960. His publications include *Independence and After*, 1962, and *America and East Asia*, 1969.

JOHN M. H. LINDBECK is director of the East Asian Institute at Columbia University. He is chairman of the Committee of Scholarly Communications with Mainland China and vice-president of the National Committee on United States-China Relations.

C. H. G. OLDHAM is a senior research fellow of the Science Policy Research Unit at the University of Sussex, England. He has previously been associated as a senior research geophysicist with the Standard Oil Company of California, and has been a fellow of the Institute of Current World Affairs and a consultant to the Scientific Directorate of the Organization for Economic Cooperation and Development in Paris. Dr. Oldham spent four years based in Hong Kong and traveling widely in

Asia studying problems of science and development. He visited China in 1964 and 1965.

The article included is reprinted with permission from the August 22, 1968, issue of *The Listener*; it was originally based on a lecture delivered to the Royal Society of Arts in London on March 25, 1968.

MERRY SELK is a member of the *Bulletin* editorial staff.

DICK WILSON was educated at Oxford University and the University of California, Berkeley. From 1958 to 1964, he lived in Hong Kong, where he was editor of the *Far Eastern Economic Review*. In that latter year, he made a tour of Communist China. Mr. Wilson currently resides in London, writing and lecturing on China and Asia. His publications include *Anatomy of China*, 1968, soon to appear in paperback.

RAY WYLIE is coordinator of the China Project for the United Church of Canada, and a member of the Consultative Committee on China, Canadian Institute of International Affairs. He served as a lecturer in English from 1965–67 at the Institute of Foreign Languages, Shanghai, China. His observations of events in China during those two years are related in the article included in this volume.

MICHAEL B. YAHUDA, who holds degrees from the School of Oriental and African Studies in London, is a lecturer in the department of politics at Southampton University. He is currently writing a dissertation on early Chinese Communist foreign policy formulation. Other articles by Mr. Yahuda appear in *China Quarterly* and the forthcoming *Year Book of World Affairs, 1969*.

Index